Icarus World Issues Series

End of Empire
5 New Works from the 15 Republics
of the Former Soviet Union

Series Editors, Roger Rosen and Patra McSharry Sevastiades

THE ROSEN PUBLISHING GROUP, INC.
NEW YORK

Published in 1994 by The Rosen Publishing Group, Inc.
29 E. 21st Street, New York, NY 10010

First Edition

Library of Congress Cataloging-in-Publication Data

End of empire : 15 new works from the 15 republics of the former
  Soviet Union / [edited by] Roger Rosen and Patra McSharry
  Sevastiades.
     p.   cm. — (Icarus world issues series)
  Includes bibliographical references and index.
  ISBN 0-8239-1802-5. — ISBN 0-8239-1803-3
     1. Former Soviet republics--Literatures--Translations into
  English. 2. Prose literature--Translations into English.
  I. Rosen, Roger. II. Sevastiades, Patra McSharry. III. Series.
PN849.R92E53   1994
808.8' 00947--dc20   94-29833
                                                               CIP

Manufactured in the United States of America

Contents

Introduction

For those of us who caught a kind of apocalyptic flu with each arctic blast from the Cold War, the demise of the USSR was as profoundly unlikely as heat stroke in Magadan in December. No one whom I've ever met, born after 1917 on either front, ever thought to witness this event in his or her lifetime. Such was the monolith that the Soviet Union had become.

Built like a bunker, and emblematically embalmed within that same shape in the center of Red Square, the Union seemed destined to endure despite the prophecies of poets, the courage of dissidents, even the machinations of Americans. Where there had once been revolutionary ardor there was now doggedness. But that massive inertia that kept the food lines snaking forward and the political machine that allowed those with the right connections to leap to the front of the queue seemed to belie all possibility for change.

And then, quite suddenly, the Empire ceased to exist. Whether one attributes this phenomenon to Brezhnev's era of stagnation, the war in Afghanistan, Gorbachev's policies of *glasnost* and *perestroika*, Reagan's star wars, the August coup, or Yeltsin's successful defense of the White House is beyond the scope of this introduction. What is certain is that the collapse of the center sent into orbits of their own the fourteen republics that, with Russia, comprised the USSR .

We conceived the idea for the subject of *Icarus* 16 more than two years ago. We wanted our readers to sample the very best work being written by indigenous authors from Armenia, Azerbaijan, Belarus, Estonia, Georgia, Kazakhstan, Kyrgyzstan, Latvia, Lithuania, Moldova, Russia, Tajikistan, Turkmenistan, Ukraine, and Uzbekistan. As one would imagine, this was an editorial challenge of no small dimension. In the former USSR, each republic had a Writer's Union that was linked to those in other republics and in Moscow through a bureaucratic network as restrictive as many of the more effective state organs. Whatever pleasures might have resulted from timely faxing from these approved organizations, however, would have been severely dampened by the knowledge that the work we were reading had been vetted and approved by *apparatchiks* or by writers who could be relied upon to denounce one of their fellows at the behest of the State. Dealing with independent writers in fifteen sovereign nations was far more exciting.

From Transcaucasia to the Baltic states, from Central Asia to Ukraine, we received letters, parcels, faxes, and hand-delivered articles written and printed in an array of alphabets and calligraphies that made us feel that we resided at the crossroads of the universe. Working with scholars and translators, we saw emerge before us the most shocking and intriguing kaleidoscope of images from an absolutely unique moment in human history. However distinctive the national voice in the hundreds of pieces we received, one element seemed common to all: No character or characteristic could be defined without the reality of Soviet existence, past or present, there as the foil against which all else could be seen. As Akbar Tursunov from Tajikistan observes perceptively in his essay "From the Ashes":

"For seventy years, Bolshevism was imposed on Soviet society. It has deep roots not only in our spiritual world but in our very psyche. As an image etched in granite, so the rules of Soviet political behavior were indelibly engraved in the conscious and subconscious of every heir to the Soviet legacy. Communism as a superpower has left the scene, but its belligerent ideology, like a radioactive dump, continues to poison our environment."

Over the years there has been much discussion about the nature of *Homo sovieticus*. We are now in a position to hear for the first time from people whose sensibilities are newly liberated, freed to be engaged by the deepest autochthonic instincts of place. Given the geopolitical realities throughout the former USSR, it is perhaps naive to believe that the opportunities for the full flowering of this expression will last for long. Whatever new mélange unfolds, however, it cannot help but to produce writing as impassioned and history-laden as the pieces in our current issue.

Roger Rosen, Editor

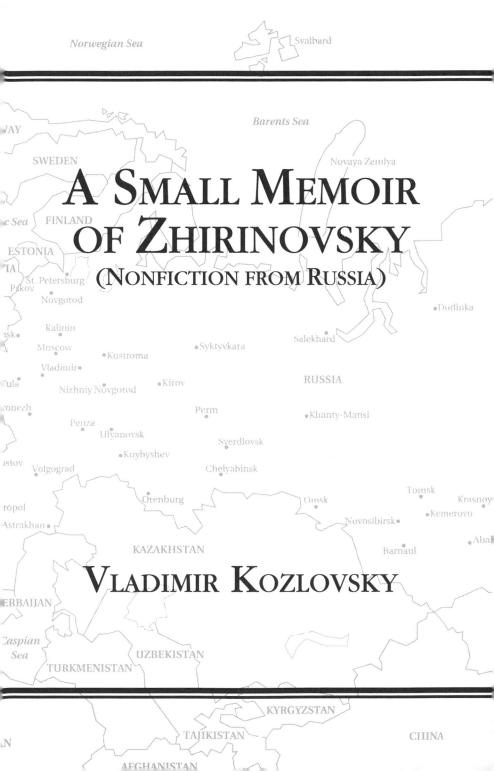

A SMALL MEMOIR
OF ZHIRINOVSKY
(NONFICTION FROM RUSSIA)

VLADIMIR KOZLOVSKY

Vladimir Zhirinovsky and Vladimir Kozlovsky

V ladimir Kozlovsky was born in Moscow in 1947. He was graduated from Moscow State University in 1970 with an undergraduate degree from the Institute of Oriental Languages. In 1973, he received a graduate degree from the Institute of Oriental Studies, USSR Academy of Sciences. In 1974, Mr. Kozlovsky, a dissident, emigrated to the United States. He received a graduate degree in political science from the City University of New York.

Mr. Kozlovsky has been an instructor of Russian at Cornell University, of Soviet subculture at Yale University, and of Soviet subculture and Indian religions at the University of Utah, Salt Lake City. In addition, he was media editor at the *New Jewish Times*.

Mr. Kozlovsky is the author, translator, or editor of roughly a dozen books. His articles and translations have appeared in *Newsday*, *Life*, and the *New Jewish Times*, among others. Mr. Kozlovsky is currently a reporter for the BBC Russian Service and a staff writer for the daily *Novoe Russkoye Slovo*.

Mr. Kozlovsky lives in Moscow and New York City.

"**O**f course, I remember Zhirinovsky," said my ex-wife, who was our schoolmate, went on to do graduate studies in Sanskrit, and is now an x-ray technician in Chicago. "A tall, handsome, blue-eyed fellow." That wasn't how most of us saw Z., who was widely considered a geek and an unstoppable motormouth; nowadays, nobody calls Z. a geek, but you still can't shut him up. It a plus for those of us who feed off other people's words, but a date with Z. must be a bummer.

We met almost thirty years ago but started talking at length only in the spring of 1991 when Z. was running for President of Russia, then still a part of the Soviet Union. He came in third, a stunning success for a political nobody, attributed by many to KGB support, which I found unlikely. Not that Z. wouldn't take KGB money—he told me that he would, gladly, inasmuch as he would without a second's hesitation take money from the Pope, AA, AAA, or UJA ("Especially from UJA," his detractors on the Russian right would giggle)—but the KGB probably thought he was too weird.

As the saying goes, Z. is a Big Tent kind of guy and will take pretty much anybody into his movement, including Jews (I saw one at his Moscow party conference in March) and gays ("Gays vote, too," he told a lesbian journalist earlier this year), although these two groups are outnumbered ten thousand to one in his Liberal Democratic Party by rabid nationalists, the disoriented dispossessed, retired colonels, bums, and a sprinkling of idealists who tend to show up in the strangest of places.

For Z., votes grow on every tree. "We need numbers, we need people," he told me in December 1992. "Please, let everybody come. We are talking about a party! If we were talking about my firm, I would of course be selective. I'd

3

need a dozen professionals, and that would be it. But a party is numbers. We need every single voter." He will get rid of the chaff when elected.

Actually, the idea is to ban (of course, "temporarily") all political parties. "Including your own?" I asked when the subject came up a week after the August 1991 Moscow coup attempt. "Of course," he said. "Of course, of course!"

I asked if his party knew about the plan. Z. didn't answer directly, and I let the matter drop. In his place, I wouldn't tell them, either. Come to think of it, I might even want to ban them, too.

In December 1993, Z.'s Liberal Democrats got almost a quarter of the popular vote for parliament—more than any other single party. A man of excruciating vulgarity and, despite three decades in Moscow, a tacky provincial accent, Z. was universally despised by the native press corps. Its squeamish members for the most part would not, as a matter of principle, interview or even mention this preposterous upstart, so it is small wonder that his victory hit them too like a ton of bricks. Moscow-based American journalists must have taken their cue from their Russian colleagues in this matter, because they missed Z.'s ascent almost completely, although in the final days of the campaign some belatedly noticed his popularity among the lower classes. By election day, his Big Mo had became unstoppable.

That so many Russians would give their vote to a pol widely thought of as being Jewish meant either that the anti-Semitism of the Russian masses had been badly exaggerated, or that the masses had reached such depths of misery that they would vote even for a Jew. Also, Z. was much more fun than his competition.

Although what I would call Eidelshteingate (the discovery that Z. was born Vladimir Eidelshtein and formally changed his family name to Zhirinovsky only in 1964) happened only last April, it was long commonly assumed that his father was Jewish. That assumption was symbolized by the now famous phrase attributed to Z., "My mother is Russian, and my father is a lawyer," although he has been claiming for years that it was pasted together from his answers to two different questions. But the phrase stuck and is now part of the Russian political vocabulary. When his detractors snicker that Z. is a "lawyer's son," everybody knows they are calling him a Jew.

I brought this up in September 1991, when we were talking in his two-room apartment, where you were greeted by a pile of worn slippers to change into. When it rains in New York, the streets are just wet; when it rains in Moscow, they are also very muddy. I've long had a theory that mud is somehow premixed into Moscow's rainwater before it hits the ground. That's why Moscovites make you take off your shoes, as if you were in a Japanese temple. Many would make an exception for a foreigner, but not Z.

In June of that year he had won about 7 million votes in the Russian presidential election, but he had little to show for his success in the way of worldly goods except a donated fax machine that wasn't working. Z. was sitting on a couch under his own campaign poster and that of the Italian Liberal Radical Party, with which he had found ideological kinship. "Say, was your father Russian or Jewish?" I asked.

It would have never crossed my mind to ask such a question back in college, where these things didn't really matter to most of us and where everyone thought Z. was Russian. But that was before the "my dad's a lawyer" business and before Z. became such a big public figure.

"My father was Russian," said Z. "They are spreading rumors that I am a KGB agent, a Jew, a stooge of the Communist Party, or whatever, to make people hate me." He even took down an old picture of his father, who died when Z. was a year old, to show me how Russian the man looked. I took a snapshot of Z. with that defense exhibit in his hands. It's just been printed in *Vanity Fair*.

"No Jews in your family at all?" "None whatsoever. What am I supposed to do?" "And what do you think of the Jews in general?" "They are O.K., but my take on the current situation is that anti-Semitism will very likely grow." "Why?" "Because the majority of the common people and Pamyat* are correct when they say that Jews have played a very active part in *perestroika* and all the recent events. Take all the new newspapers—70 percent of their writers and editors are Jewish."

So lots of people were surprised a couple of years ago when the story broke that in the late 1980s Z. himself was something of a Jewish activist, albeit very briefly, having joined the Jewish cultural association Shalom. It certainly was news to me. I came to Z. with the intention of asking, "Say it ain't so." Instead, I got a full confession.

This time we talked in his new office in a slum-like building on the once charming Rybnikov Lane, which in December 1992 looked like a South Bronx movie set. Z. sat surrounded by such artifacts as two flak jackets, one heavy and one light, two books by Jean-Marie Le Pen acquired on a visit to Paris where he was introduced to the French rightist, an olive green Iraqi uniform, and a hideous oil painting of some horsemen presented to him by his hosts on a visit to Baghdad. Also in evidence was the emblem of Z.'s party, a map of Russia that includes Poland and Alaska.

"What's the symbolism of the flak jackets?" I asked. "It's my connection to the army. I find them sympathetic, they find me sympathetic. Here's another gift, a helmet. See the white helmet behind that photograph? I got it from the Leningrad Metallurgic Plant."

"What about the uniform?" "When I was in Iraq, I liked their uniforms. They are, like, good-looking. And unpretentious. So I got the uniform as a present."

---

*Pamyat—an anti-Semitic extreme nationalist organization.

My next question was along the lines of, "Are you now or have you ever been a member of Shalom?" Z., whom many people now consider a Nazi, confirmed that he had indeed been a member of that Jewish organization; he was even elected to its board and headed four sections.

As he explained it, back in the late 1980s, when Z. didn't yet have his own political party, he would join any organization and climb on any soapbox just to make himself known. He spoke at some Armenian rallies, some Turkish ones, some Ossetian ones. He went to Pamyat rallies, although a whole year passed before they let him climb on their soapbox. "But it doesn't mean that I was pro-Armenian, pro-Ossetian, pro-Pamyat, or anti-Semitic, or a Zionist," he protested. "Before my own party gestated, I went to all political events; otherwise I would have never formed my own party."

That didn't explain, though, why Shalom was the only outfit in which Z. held a position of prominence; he certainly was not on the board of any other political organization. Then the Israelis reported that in 1983 Z. was briefly interested in emigration to their country. Finally, Eidelshteingate broke out.

Some liberal journalists in Moscow were gleefully predicting that the discovery in Kazakh archives of Z.'s birth certificate bearing the very Jewish-sounding name Eidelshtein would blow him out of the water. But nothing happened. In a few days, the story died.

The mainstream media, largely controlled by Russia's democrats, would not use Z.'s Jewishness as a stick to beat him with, while the few extreme nationalist publications came to see him as their last great white hope and also held their peace. Getting away with such a handicap in Russian politics is no small feat, especially for Z., who is trying to corner the market on Russian nationalism, but he has somehow pulled it off.

Recently, I went to see Victor Novoseltsev, deputy editor

of LDP's newspaper *Pravda Zhirinovskogo.* "I used to be a hippie," he told me, and conspiratorially showed me his old I.D. photograph with shoulder-length hair, "but then I came to like discipline." "What about that Eidelshtein business?" I asked. The former hippie shrugged it off as a fabrication of the Kazakh intelligence service, which certainly is no fan of Z.'s because he wants to make Kazakhstan part of Russia. There are many places and countries that Z. would like to incorporate, including Alaska.

"I am sorry," Z. told me a couple of years ago, "but Alaska is Russian." I said forget it. Z., who is quite flexible, said he would go for Alaska only "if America collapses." "No way is it going to collapse," I said. "Well," he said, "if it doesn't collapse, the Americans can keep it."

When there was still a Soviet Union, Z. and I haggled once over Turkey, which he hates because back in the late 1960s when he worked there as a translator, the Turkish police busted him for something; he claims it was for giving some Soviet pins to local kids. The pins supposedly bore a visage of the Russian poet Pushkin, whom the Turks took for Karl Marx and gave Z. a hard time for spreading Soviet propaganda. It was rumored at our school that Z. was arrested for espionage, which I found hard to believe. In those years I knew him rather as a dissident of sorts, always talking pluralism and reforms; he would never get a security clearance to spy.

Whatever the case may be, Z., who is big on grudges, has never since stopped disliking the Turks and told me he wanted them in Russia's sphere of influence. He said that in exchange the United States could have Lithuania. "No way," I said, "Turkey is a member of NATO." "O.K." he said, "but then we'll keep Kaunas," which is Lithuania's second largest city.

The way things have worked out, the United States still has Turkey but Z. lost Lithuania. Many Russians unhappy with this outcome have flocked to a politician who once promised to bury radioactive waste on the border with the Baltic states and put in a giant fan that would blow in their direction.

Here's a splendid example of life imitating art; there was a joke in the US after the Chernobyl nuclear disaster: "What is Russia's secret weapon? A giant fan!" I bet Z. never heard that one, so he must come up with the fan idea on his own. "Are you kidding?" I asked, "And where are you going to find such a big fan in this country?" "Consider it a joke," he laughed.

Z. says things like that for their shock value, and thus far this approach has done wonders for him. "Don't tell me to change what I am doing! So far, I've been right all the way." He isn't going to plant any giant fans or father a child in Russia's every region (his latest campaign pledge), but promising these things keeps him in the media spotlight. Z. is Russia's first media politician; for that matter, he is its first professional pol. He lives politics, he breathes politics, he had been preparing himself for big-time politics from his humble beginnings in dusty Almaty and through joyless college years spent sulking in his dorm room on Lenin Hills, unloved, unwanted, and therefore with a lot of time on his hands to read and reflect on his miseries and future greatness (his autobiography has been compared to *Mein Kampf*, although much of it sounds rather like parts of *Oliver Twist*).

"They should write the truth, but they are lying, lying, lying," he told me once, complaining about his treatment by Russian journalists. "One day they call me an anti-Semite, another, a Zionist, or a KGB agent, or a Communist Party agent, although I have nothing to do with the Communists, or the Jews, or the KGB. I've done everything on my own. I came to Moscow on my own, I chose a school on my own, I was a straight A student on my own, because I was hungry and angry, I was poor. If I had the kind of money my classmates had, I wouldn't be such a good student! But I was destitute, destitute!"

Well, now he has shown us all. Z. is a study in overcompensation.

A demagogue and political prankster, he doesn't believe 90 percent of the things he says, but there is one issue about which he seems genuinely passionate: Z. is a geopolitical visionary (his faction even got the lower house of parliament to set up a special "committee on geopolitics," squandering part of its clout on a totally ludicrous project).

Former Soviet diplomat 32-year-old Aleksey Mitrofanov, who is foreign minister in Z.'s shadow cabinet, once declared in print that "our aim is world domination," but Z. has always said that he doesn't want the whole thing, just parts of it that are historically Russian. It is a huge chunk of real estate that on occasion includes Turkey and India, but on the other hand he is willing to get out of the Western hemisphere and some other places.

"What kind of relationship with America do you envision?" I asked back in 1991. "We must have a partnership with America," he said, "and agree on spheres of influence. Ideologically, we must leave Latin America. There was Nicaragua, there was Cuba, some other ventures—no more. We shouldn't spread around our ideology. We shouldn't be a source of anti-American sentiments anywhere. We would want the same thing from America: that it wouldn't be a source of anti-Russian sentiments. This is all. Same with Japan and Germany. If we—Russia, Japan, Germany, and America—agree on spheres of influence, the world will be more stable, although some small countries will be unhappy."

There will be a lot of unhappy small countries should Z. ever see his dreams come true. He wants most of Estonia, although the natives would be allowed to keep their capital of Tallinn (without its port). Latvians, on the other hand, wouldn't get to keep even their own city-state ("Half of its people are Russians," he told me, "so it'll forever be with us").

Ukrainians will get to keep their three westernmost provinces; as Z. put it, "they can choke on them." But he predicts "an eternal enmity between Poland and this small West Ukrainian Republic." This is just a fragment of his plan, which he recites with great excitement.

True, sometimes Z. can be confusing. I went to one of the rallies that he holds every first Saturday of the month at the Sokolniki Metro station. Instead of talking "partnership" with America and condominium with the West, he was screaming at the rabid nationalists, the disoriented dispossessed, retired colonels, bums, and other usual suspects who come to listen to his speeches, "You are being slowly destroyed! You must realize it! And understand who is doing it! The West is doing it!"

Dividing spheres of influence with Z. promises to be a tough undertaking. He is Russia's second most popular politician after Yeltsin.

BLIAKHA, OR AFTER CHERNOBYL
(FICTION FROM BELARUS)

ANDREY M. FEDARENKO

Andrey Fedarenko was born in the Gomel region of Belarus in 1964. In 1983 he was graduated from the Mazyrsky Polytechnical Institute. He served in the Soviet Army from 1983 until 1984 and subsequently was a transportation worker in Kalinkovichy. Mr. Fedarenko was graduated from the School of Library Sciences of the Minsk Cultural Institute in 1990.

Mr. Fedarenko is the author of two books. His short stories and articles have been published widely in the magazines and newspapers of Belarus. Mr. Fedarenko was awarded the annual literary prize by the weekly *LiM*, and one of his short stories was named the Best Short Story of the Year by the International Fund of Peace/Moscow Center for Philanthropy. He was a member of the Writers Union of the Soviet Union from 1990 until it disbanded. Mr. Fedarenko is currently the editorial director of the department of culture and science at the journal *Polymya*.

Mr. Fedarenko and his wife, Alina, live in Minsk.

Misfortune makes everyone equal.

It was only after Chernobyl that Bliakha* recognized that he too was a human being. Who would ever have imagined that the old man himself, at one time the best farmer in the village, would limp over to ask Bliakha to help him slaughter a pig tomorrow? And the way he put it: "Vic, I'm already done for, you see it yourself . . . I've had my day . . . " He even remembered my real name, Bliakha thought.

The farmer had brought a bottle of wine with him. Of course, Bliakha might have reminded him of something, reminded him that when he was a little boy the old man would not allow him to sing Christmas carols in his house, while letting others perform and paying them more than anybody else did—a ruble to each of them. To him, the old man had said, "What, you're still crawling around under foot?" Bliakha might also have reminded him how his wife had fabricated stories that he had stolen some buckets or something from her, when he had not even been at home at the time but at the dentist's in Naroulia. Yes, he might have reminded him, but, well, he didn't. He only patted the old man on the shoulder and said, "Oh *bliakha,* I'll come, what else is there to do . . ."

Bliakha was a gentle, harmless man who, before Chernobyl, when the village was still alive, would do any kind of work for anyone in exchange for a drink. In the village, however, people avoided him and disliked him, as they generally dislike failures in Belarusan villages. How could you get along with someone like that: a puny, drunken convict? He had grown up without a father, never listened to his mother, had done poorly in school,

---

bliakha—literally, a thin plate of metal. However, the word is frequently used as a mild profanity in Belarus.

and in the eighth grade had stolen a moped and been put behind bars for a year and a half. While he was in prison, his mother had died. It seems he had had some problems in jail; he may have been beaten, because he was declared disabled upon his release. Bliakha got along somehow on his meager monthly pension of sixteen rubles. He lived by himself—no girl would marry him, and he was afraid to get too close himself.

Bliakha came back to life when, after Chernobyl, the military came to his village and started dousing houses with water from fire engines and sinking concrete posts into the ground on the outskirts of the village to stretch barbed wire between them. Bliakha came back to life when buses began rolling from behind the wire from neighboring villages as if fleeing a war; when trucks, loaded with people and livestock, started moving; when villagers, however slowly, began leaving voluntarily. He helped people load the trucks, saw them off, visited the cemetery with them to say goodbye to the deceased, and listened to their crying, wailing, and cursing. He even put in an accusing word of his own: "There, they did it . . ." The people readily offered him drinks. They looked at him and talked to him as if he, a stranger, were their closest relative. For the first time he read in their eyes not disdain, but something more like guilt, and the very love that he had missed so much in his life.

By winter, only an old man with his wife and a single old woman, a paramedic whom Bliakha helped eagerly because she offered him pure alcohol to drink, remained in their village, which had been small to begin with. Bliakha's neighbor was the last to leave. After seeing him off that day, Bliakha climbed over the fence in the evening, pulled the boards from a window, removed a window pane and entered the neighbor's house, without even realizing why he was doing it. First, he sat at a table, the same table at which the landlady had cried recently while he shared a drink with the man of the house. There was a wardrobe with both doors open, two empty beds with patched mattresses, and two armchairs turned over along the wall—a sign for a good and speedy return. Bliakha did not look for anything, nor did he want to steal anything. It was simply interesting: There had been people living here, and, suddenly, the place was empty. Later he would break into other people's houses, but he never took anything.

In the evenings he occasionally ventured into the "zone," the neighboring abandoned villages. It was even more interesting there. There were houses with decorative rugs on the walls, with television sets, refrigerators, and wardrobes full of clothes . . . If not for a strong odor inside, one would think that people were still living here, that they had just stepped out to the garden.

From these visits Bliakha brought back a radio set (even though he had a similar set of his own), a bottle of vegetable oil, and a nylon jacket with snap fasteners. Later he stopped his visits; they were no longer interesting, they had become frightening. Once he barely saved himself from packs of dogs, which of late had begun roaming wild through the villages, tearing up everything in sight. Recently they tore the farmer's dog Tuz to pieces, right under the old man's window. Another time, soldiers caught Bliakha near the barbed wire fence and punched him. And still another time, while returning from the "zone" at dusk, he saw two cars with their lights out near a house, and heard some muffled voices. Bliakha sat in the bushes, afraid to make a sound. He saw men carrying items from the house and loading them into their cars. After that he lost the desire to visit the "zone."

So it was that, after Chernobyl, a drunk nicknamed Bliakha became a man. And now, as if he were a real solid, practical family man, he was asked to help slaughter a pig.

He woke up late, looked out the window, and only then realized why he had slept so well: It was snowing. Bliakha dressed, put on his coat, pulled down his winter cap, finished on an empty stomach the rest of the wine the old man brought for him yesterday, and shuffled outside. There was so much snow that he could barely open the door. It was still falling, with a pleasant smell, white, thick, and fluffy. The street, as lifeless as it was, with no tracks upon the roadway and no smoke above the white roofs, was winterly festive, with white trees along the fences and wires on poles sagging from the weight of the snow.

At the intersection of the street and the Naroulia highway, Bliakha saw a car with both front doors open. A young man wearing a brown leather jacket and athletic pants was standing at the car, shamelessly watering the snow. Military automobiles, police cars, and several other types of vehicles were running along the highway every day now, so this was nothing new for Bliakha. Looking down at his feet and feigning disinterest in everything around him, he let the car slip away from his sight.

"Hey, man, just a minute," he heard, in Russian, from behind him. He turned and saw the young Russian buttoning his jacket and coming toward him. The man had a buzz cut that he probably got before he joined the military. He came closer, staring with round blank eyes, so that Bliakha shrank in fear from his gaze. He had seen a lot of people in his life with such eyes. These people always needed some warming up. They always wanted to hit somebody for no reason at all, beat up somebody and watch what happened. Bliakha remembered similar eyes from his interrogations, from the jail, railway stations, and from the Naroulia joint.

Without a word, the young man kicked Bliakha in the chest. Bliakha was spun around and flung headlong into the snow toward the fence. Despite the blow, he managed to jump quickly to his feet and run to the nearest house. Luckily, the gate was unlocked. He went in and, gasping for air, hid behind a gate post. Then he heard the engine of the automobile.

Bliakha sat down right on the snow with his knees trembling. It was lucky for him that the man did not follow him. He could have been killed here, and nobody would even have looked for him. Still, it turned out well—only his chest was hurting and his neck was hard to turn. Bliakha did not harbor much of a grudge against the man. He was a little hurt because it all happened at home, in his own village, on his own street.

A hungry young hog was knocking against its feeding trough. The heavy snow was coming down and Bliakha had not yet arrived. The old man's wife had jumped out of bed early, at about five o'clock in the morning, fired up the stove, washed her cast-iron kettles, steamed the pork tub, rinsed the trough for the intestines, gone up to the loft and thrown down a bundle of straw. And now while shoveling the snow around the pigsty, she kept running to the street after each shovelful, cursing not only slaughterers like Bliakha but also snow that falls when nobody needs it. The old man, feeling a little better today, was also hobbling around. He crushed some salt in the box with his hammer, put in the shed sharpened knives, a rope, and a bucket with a cup to collect blood, and filled the blowtorch with gasoline. He saw that the old lady was nervous. She didn't even want to talk, so he too was guiltily silent.

But, come to think of it, why was he guilty? Was it because he had become ill, or that the snow was falling and they would have to come up with a way to burn off the pig's bristles—that is, if somebody would still slaughter it today? Had the old man always been like this? No, during his life he had kept his distance, wouldn't come within a mile of people like Bliakha or any other kind of "helpers." Would he ever have slaughtered his pig on a snowy day like today? No, he always selected a quiet frosty day with a little snow on the ground. He would talk to his pig, scratch its belly and behind its ears, loop a cord over the pig's hind leg, tie the cord carefully to the gate post and then push the pig down. He always aimed at the "apple," the center of the throat. His pig would never squeal like other people's would; it would only wheeze and choke, each time producing more blood. He burned off the pig's bristles by himself. First he burned some straw to impart a pleasant aroma to the skin, and then used a gasoline blowtorch or a gas burner, making the pigskin nice and yellow. It did not matter that he did it all by himself.

By this time of the day the pig would have been cleaned of bristles, thoroughly scraped, washed, and ready for butchering. But then again, properly speaking, who would ever slaughter such a small summer hog if it weren't for Chernobyl, which before the disaster was a place no one had even heard of. It was good that we were smart enough not to move anywhere, the old man thought. They used to come and ask him and his wife to move to their son's town, promising to register them to obtain any size dwelling, and then threatening to move them by force sooner or later. It is a good thing that we didn't listen, the old man thought, because they have stopped coming now—nobody needs anybody any longer.

Naturally, the old man and his wife never believed in any Chernobyl disaster or radiation; 90 percent of the people who were moved or left on their own didn't. One couldn't believe in such nonsense.

Radiation, which had been neither heard nor seen before by anyone, did not come by itself; it was something produced by people, directly related to them. It wasn't radiation that drove people from their homes, invented the "zone" and put a fence around it; it wasn't radiation that kept farmers from making hay and rejected their milk, cows, and pigs. All this was done by people, people like the old man and his wife.

They had gotten used to defending themselves from

others—before, during, and after the war. They had to live quietly, not bother anybody, and endure everything silently. Then nobody and nothing would bother them, neither people nor radiation.

There was one bad thing: Their son and their granddaughter stopped coming from the town to visit them. Their son never invited them to see him as he did before. It wasn't that he thought radiation might harm the granddaughter, but because everybody acted that way; nobody ever came to see them. The old man and his wife pointed out that even the paramedic's niece came with a little girl to visit her on October holidays.

How could they not see their granddaughter, now that the old man had physically gone to pieces? Now he says openly that this is his last year and the old lady will not live forever, either.

So they seized upon a reason to visit their son and granddaughter; not empty-handed, but with fresh pork. "Besides, what the devil do we need the pig for? First we have to feed it, and then we don't even know what to do with it. Life has passed us by, we don't need our little farm. It's enough to keep the three chickens we still have, and who knows if they'll pull through. Look at our Tuz, killed by wild dogs . . . the only thing left was the doghouse and a rusted chain attached to a post . . ."

By now they had resigned themselves to the fact that nobody would come and that it was too late to slaughter the pig today. When the old lady took some food to the pig, Bliakha showed up all rumpled and fussy.

"Where is the pig?" he said. "Oh *bliakha*, I thought I was too early."

A good farmer might say, about this particular slaughter, "Well, at least we choked the life out of that pig somehow."

The pig was small, but stiff, resilient. It was not sleepy or awkward, like well-fed pigs, with clumsy legs. Those are easy to slaughter. When the pig was let out into the fenced-in yard, it walked around, did not find the trough, snorted angrily with its snout in the snow, and tried to go back into the pigsty, but the old lady closed the door and began scratching its belly. The old man was not in the yard. He pushed the end of a cord to Bliakha between the fence boards, saying, "Use the cord, as I did."

Bliakha waved him away. He stretched out his arm with the knife in his hand, circled the pig, aimed, and suddenly threw himself upon it with desperate swiftness, grabbing it by the foreleg and throwing it onto its back. Before the knife was lodged inside the throat the stunned animal jumped back to its feet with the kind of terrible squeal that fills people's ears and makes their blood run cold.

"Oh, Lord!" cried the old lady in despair, not knowing what to do with herself. With a squeal, and bloody foam pouring from its open mouth, the pig struck the pigsty door with its head, and standing on its hind legs crawled up the door, scraping at the iron latch with its forehooves. Jumping toward the pig, Bliakha pushed his entire blade into the open wound two or three times and pulled the knife out. Only then blood rushed from the wound, the squealing stopped, and the pig fell slowly down from the door. It wheezed, contracted convulsively, and soiled itself in the blood that poured out all over the snow. It jerked its legs so frequently and with such force that nobody dared come near it. They didn't collect any blood, not a drop.

"Be thankful the pig stood up at the door!" the old man smiled, for some reason taking off his hat when the pig was finally still. "They do stand up sometimes. You know, once . . ."

"I know—once you missed the mark, too!" interrupted Bliakha, justifying himself. His right hand was still trembling, and tiny drops of blood fell on the snow from the knife.

After burning off the pig's bristles, they were drenched

in sweat. The snow was not fluffy anymore. It was dry from the wind, which kept putting out the fire on the burning straw. They had to sweep the snow off the pig. The blowtorches worked poorly, so some spots didn't get enough heat, while others got too much. When they turned the pig over they tore the skin on its belly. The old lady could barely control her emotions. They washed the pig, cut off the head and set it on the snow to drain the blood. When they started butchering it, they tore an intestine. The old lady cried and shouted at her husband, "What are you doing?" She didn't say anything to Bliakha, as if he weren't even there.

Somehow or other they butchered the pig, carried the pieces into the work room, and placed them on the tables lining the wall. In the main room of the house, the old lady began frying pork on the gas range while the old man, after wiping his hands with a towel, sliced some bread and wiped off some shot glasses. Bliakha, feeling guilty the whole day and seeing that he could not please the old lady, asked her, "Where do you have some warm water to wash my hands?"

"Go wipe your hands on the snow, I don't have anybody to carry the water . . ."

When they sat down at the table, it wasn't even four o'clock, but nothing could be seen through the window. The wind was blowing, making noise like grain striking the window panes. Bliakha squeezed in at the end of the table by the window, and the old man sat at the opposite end, with his back to the inside of the house. The old lady brought in the trough with the intestines and began splashing water in the trough without even glancing at the table.

"Come and sit with us, missus," Bliakha said as politely as he could, while filling the shot glasses.

"You don't need me! Drink faster, and . . . I still have work enough until midnight."

"Oh *bliakha*, why are you all so angry? Why? Is your life so bad? Look at me: I didn't have any life and I'm not crying! Am I right, old man?"

"It's true . . ."

"We're such a sorry lot—we're in it so deep already that this is really piddling! Oh, *bliakha* to all this radiation! Am I right?"

"It is all true, we've had our day . . ."

"Just go ahead and drink. Enough with the '*bliakhas*' already." The old lady left the intestines and went out into the work room. It was already dark, as though late at night. She lit a lamp, pushed the pork tub in from the shed, and began cutting and salting the pork fat, which cooled quickly, and placing it back in the tub.

The old lady was angry at Bliakha, not at her life. God grant every woman a chance to live as she had with the old man. She was angry that everything had become senseless, stupid, with no one knowing what to do any longer. With each day, everything was getting worse and worse.

Why wouldn't you sit at the table, drink, have a bite to eat, and sing songs—if there were nothing hanging over your head; if everything were leisurely, peaceful; if one knew that the old man was well and that their son would visit them on his days off; if there was nothing to worry about; if she were healthy and spry as she had been before. As it was, night had fallen and nothing had gotten done yet. She had completely forgotten about the chickens, which people were now afraid to let outside. They had been sitting hungry since this morning. The old lady stopped salting pork, filled a glove with millet and went to feed the chickens.

The wind snatched the door out of her hand. The wind was dry and cold. It blew all over the place, making snowdrifts that seemed to be reaching toward the sky. The middle of the yard was clear, as though it had been swept clean, while substantial drifts had built up along the fence, the barn, and the woodshed. Shielding herself from the wind, the old lady came to the end of the yellow rectangle cast by the light from the house, and here, along the line between the areas of dark and light, a long black shadow shifted right under her feet. In front of her, near the woodshed where they had worked on the pig, she saw several other shadows and heard a sound through the wind as if paws were raking the snow.

She immediately remembered the wild shriek from under the window when the dogs were tearing their Tuz to pieces, and she and the old man had been afraid even to walk out of the house. She shouted from fear, and the shadows, whining their displeasure, slipped behind the woodshed, deeper into the dark. Their attention was caught not by the shout but by a pale, strange light which, passing through the snow from the street, reflected off the barn wall, and by a hollow roar barely audible in the wind. The old lady, forgetting her chickens and moving backward, returned to the porch; the gate squeaked, pushing the snow away, and somebody entered the yard.

Bliakha, sitting at the window, pushed the curtain aside, trying to make out anything. The only thing to be seen outside was the snowstorm.

"Dogs, carrion . . . They fell into the habit," the old man said, rolling fried pork around inside his mouth between his bare gums. He was a bit tight. "They smell it!"

"Yes, *bliakha*, old man, there are enough hunters even for your pitiful pork," laughed Bliakha, drunk and quite pleasant. "Man, listen to me . . ." He tapped his fingernail on the empty bottle. "How about another?"

"It's up to my old lady; I . . ." hesitated the old man. Then he agreed, and went to open the door to the work room. It wouldn't budge. He pushed with more strength, knocked on it, leaned against it with his shoulder, and then sighed and stretched his arms out in a futile gesture . . .

Both the old man and Bliakha thought that the old lady

had locked the door on purpose, so they wouldn't bother her any more. They sat a while longer and talked. Bliakha had a smoke and had put his coat and cap on when the latch opened and the old lady, half-dead from fright, tumbled inside the main room, wailing and wringing her hands.

"Oh, people! What did I do to deserve such a fate! Hey, old man, run to the police . . . He even took the thigh, ribs, and the fat! He had a backpack!"

While they were drinking, a thief had entered the work room, terrorized the old lady who was already numb from fear, closed the latch carefully so that nobody could come out from the main room, and had taken whatever he wanted. Now all three of them stood in the work room, not knowing what to do.

"Why didn't you say anything?" Bliakha shouted at the old lady, who stood next to the old man. They were both bent over with age.

"What if he had hit me over the head?"

Suddenly, dogs yelping, growling, and a man's voice and foul language could be heard from the yard closer to the street. The sounds, rolling forward like a ball, became easier to hear, and clear. The ball was rolling into the yard, toward the house, closer to the door.

The old lady began wailing again and ran into the main room. Bliakha grabbed a knife from the table and stood at the door, while the old man pulled a flail from behind some bags in the corner.

The ball, squealing and growling, calmed down a bit, as though it had struck the wall. There came a knock at the door, which was unlocked, and someone shouted in Russian, with a high-pitched, frightened, childlike voice, "Ma'am, ma'am, please—anybody!"

Bliakha shouted back, "I'll kill you, don't you say a word!" He opened the door a little.

*   *   *

A young man tumbled into the work room. He slid his back down the door jamb and came to rest on the floor, squeezing his arms, bloodied up to the elbows, between his legs. Not a single spot on him was left unscathed. His short leather coat was full of holes, torn to pieces. Bloody gashes showed through his shredded athletic pants. Blood was running down his nose and lips onto his chin. His face was white, without a trace of blood left in it. The young man sat up and looked around the work room with round, deeply sunken eyes and whispered, "Ma'am, please, a bandage . . . there is a first aid kit in the car."

He didn't even notice that his "ma'am" was not in the work room. Bliakha, without taking his eyes off the man, dropped his knife-wielding hand.

"Well, should we bandage you up?" he said, squinting his eyes. "So this is *your* work? Where is the meat?"

"You, you sweet people, I beg of you," whispered the young man, curling himself into a ball as Bliakha did in the mornings.

"Where is the meat?"

"The dogs carried it off." Excited and pleased, the old man came closer, without letting the flail out of his hands.

"Here's your bandage!" Bliakha kicked the man in the side.

"People! I beg you!" the young man shrieked wildly—where did the strength come from?—and then fell, face down.

"That's for stealing!" laughed the old man.

A bloodstain was getting darker near the door jamb where the young man had been sitting. Bliakha bent over him saying, "Well, let me see," and pulled the man's hands from between his legs. "Oh *bliakha*, he's passed out," he said, dumbfounded. "Look here, old man, how he has been torn up all over . . . nothing but raw flesh."

The old man looked and touched him. "I hope he doesn't die," he scratched his neck. "All these dogs have rabies . . .

Maybe we should get the police or an ambulance."

"What should we do?" Bliakha mused. He felt sorry now for kicking the young man. With the kick, not only had he lost all his resentment and his grudge against the young man, but some drunk, silly pity, some humble affection had rushed to his head, as if the young man were his son. To draw away the pity—and to keep from crying, for that matter—Bliakha wanted to have a smoke, but he could not find his matches. He turned quickly as though his heels were burning.

"What should we do, eh, old man?" he repeated. "Let him stay here until the morning and then we'll see. What else is there to do? Oh *bliakha*, I feel sorry for the young carrion. Listen, old man, call your wife and drag him into the main room. Maybe we should put some bandages on him or something. I will run over to the paramedic's house, or if not, I will run to the post where the soldiers are. Do you hear me?"

"He brought it on himself. He shouldn't steal," said the old man, standing still.

"Hey, old man, who was I talking to? I'll be right back!"

He jumped outside, excited, drunk, full of energy, squeezing the knife in his hand. He had run almost to the gate, he could even see the outline of the light-colored car on the street, when in his excitement he ran into a black beast gnawing something at the gate. The creature, with a gleeful growl, snapped at him and bit into his thigh. Bliakha still had time to jump away, but he slipped and fell on all fours, and swung his knife into emptiness. He even had time to think, "Are they dogs?" But they were already upon him, gnawing at his legs, tearing at the back of his light nylon coat, coming closer to his face and throat. He tried to push them away, run away and somehow get back to the door . . .

He shouted something, but his shouts were drowned in

the wild yelping and mad squealing of an excited pack that had tasted blood—a pack that, as if surrounding a hated animal during the hunt, attacked, tore, gnawed, and tried to bite into its prey's throat, without waiting for so much as a sign from the hunter.

There was no one to help, protect, or save him. Only the wind swirled the snow up from below, as if it were the end of the world.

Translated from the Belarusan
by Russell and Alex Zavistovich

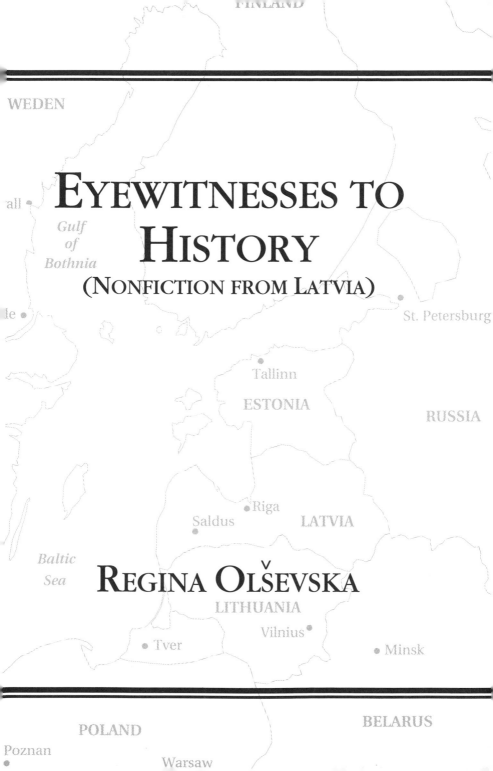

EYEWITNESSES TO HISTORY
(NONFICTION FROM LATVIA)

REGINA OLŠEVSKA

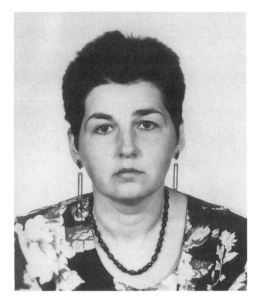

Regina Olševska was born in 1958 in Cesis, Latvia. She received a degree in philology and philosophy from the University of Latvia. Subsequently, she worked as an elementary school teacher of Latvian language and literature.

Ms. Olševska is the editor of *Gramato Apskats*, the Latvian analog of *Publishers Weekly*. She also prepares translations of German and French literature. Ms. Olševska has translated the poems of Rimbaud, Verlaine, and Verhoeven, among others, which have appeared in the magazine *Avots* and the newspaper *Nakts*. She has published poems in publications including *Liesma* and *Latvijas Jaunatne*.

Ms. Olševska is married and has two children. She currently lives in Riga.

It is hard to live at a time when history is happening; it is hard to write about history that is happening, to me and to all of us in Latvia, at this moment. It is hard because there is no place from which to step back, from which to see clearly the crossroads where we stood, to see the road that we chose and started upon, the one we are continuing on and will continue on, some faster, some slower, but, nonetheless, all of us together.

It happened four years ago. In May 1990. Latvia adopted its Declaration of Independence. My son was born. In an already independent Latvia. I had to look at many things differently. I. All the people in the new nation. And people elsewhere in the world, close by, far, and very far from Latvia. News about Latvia spread throughout the world. News of the world came into Latvia without censorship and commentary. Radio Free Europe. CNN. Satellite television. Video. Newspapers, magazines, in all the languages of the world for everyone who can read them. Freedom of choice—to read a book that was forbidden, or a magazine about which you have heard from friends. To read the lines, not between the lines. To travel to other lands or not to travel. Not because you are not allowed but because you don't want to, have no money, don't like the time of year. Freedom to say what you think, find out what you want, hear words that make you sweat, as in the olden days.

My son has cut his first teeth. In Riga—barricades. January 1991. Barricades are being built—near government buildings, near the television and radio stations. Right on the streets. Tractors, trucks, vans, lumber trucks, buses. Bonfires in the streets and squares. People are in Riga from all over Latvia. Farmers. They are warming their frozen hands, brewing tea. Protecting independence.

Everything that sets one person apart from another vanishes: farmer from city dweller, one generation from the other. What separates them is not important, you are I, and they are we. We will never be like this again in Latvia, this close to history. And the measure by which we will later measure ourselves and others will never again reach such a high level. Changes that are hard to see. Those exist in every person. Just as a stone that has fallen into a brook makes the stream leave its old course and find a new one.

My son is beginning to walk by himself now. Latvia—is beginning to live. Without Moscow's hand on its shoulder and in its pocket. Gasoline crisis. Heating crisis. Monetary reform. One. After that . . .—another. Russian rubles. Latvian rubles, American dollars, *lats*.* Thousands of people calculate the rate of exchange in their heads. Expensive? Cheap? Thousands of people lose their savings. Inflation. Currency exchange takes place at the farmers' market, railroad station, store, newspaper stand, church. Pharisees and money changers. Money counterfeiters.

Asian restaurants. Chinese cuisine. Italian furniture. French china and fashion. Arab perfumes. Jackets from Taiwan. Juices from Poland. Hamburgers and McDonalds. Bistro. American pizzas. Frankfurters. Scandinavian humanitarian aid. English tea and Spanish boots. Sneakers. Bananas and avocado. Used cars from all over Europe and parts from America. Unused hypodermic needles from Sweden. Russian television. Latvian passports. Free press. Free prices. Fixed salaries. Elected parliament. A president.

The poor inhabitants—doctors, teachers, actors, professors, college instructors. Fundraising for cultural undertakings for the theaters, for libraries, for orphans. Charity. Sumptuous receptions. The King of Denmark in Latvia.

---

lats—Latvian currency.

The President of America. Beggars near churches, near underground crossings. Near grocery stores. Children abandoned by their parents. Children who sell newspapers, wash cars. Children who ask for gifts of mercy. Drug addicts. The weapons marketplace. The theft of colored metals: pipes, cables, commemorative plaques, sculptures. Copper. Bronze. Buyers. Dollars. Trains and elevators stop. Unlimited trafficking in alcohol.

Work is halted in the plants and factories. Joblessness. Collective farms are liquidated. Land reform. Return of houses to former owners. Rehabilitation of the victims of Stalin's repression.

My son has begun to talk. Latvia has adopted a language law. In Latvia one has to speak, read, understand Latvian. Contracts have to be drawn, decisions made, buyers served, patients treated in Latvian. Russian disappears from stores, movie ads, from street signs. But it does not disappear from the streets and from school syllabuses. The first Latvian song festival without Russian songs. Without the Soviet Red Army band. The honor guard at the Freedom Statue in Riga, flowers placed at its base without fear. Demonstrations that are not dispersed. The Latvian flag that does not get yanked down. Songs that are not forbidden. Places where one can stand undisturbed. Conversations that are not monitored. The native tongue that is not ridiculed.

The building of hotels. The Old Town restored. New stores, restaurants, cafes. Tourists from America, Germany, Sweden. Foreign embassies. Cultural contacts. Joint ventures. Banks. Companies. Expensive foreign cars, driven by officials and men with shaved heads and tattoos on their arms. The movement of stolen cars. Weapons' and narcotics' trafficking. Robberies. Coercion. Bribery. Lines for free food for the homeless. The opportunity to study abroad. Grants. Scholarships. People who give money to the arts and culture. The rebirth of churches. An increase in the number of faithful. The return of property to the churches. Religious instruction in the schools. Freedom of religion.

The destruction of the farmers. Ham from Finland, margarine from Germany, fish from Denmark, meat from Argentina. Milk is poured into the ditches, no one is buying it. The farmers are blockading the roads to cars that bring food products into Latvia. Unemployment compensation. Subsidies for children. A high rate of unemployment in Latvian towns.

My son asks question after question. Latvia is waiting for answers from its government and ministers. From the party officials. Freedom of speech. The freedom to criticize the government, to join a party, to leave a party, not to join any party. The freedom to live in a state that is free of the Communist Party. College students hold a funeral for scientific communism. A black coffin is carried through the streets of Riga. Lenin's statue is cleared out of Riga's main street. Lenin's writings—out of the bookcases. Out of the course syllabuses. The streets regain their old names.

Sometimes I lose patience with my son. Russia is taking its army out of Latvia, Lithuania, and Estonia. My son will not have to serve in it. Latvia has its own army. Its own anthem to sing and its own borders to guard. So that the Russian army may not someday return.

Translated from the Latvian
by Regina Gravers

LIFE IN A DREAM
(FICTION FROM UZBEKISTAN)

UTKIR HASHIMOV

U tkir Hashimov was born in 1941 in Tashkent, Uzbekistan. In 1964, he graduated from Tashkent State University. In that year he began work as editor-in-chief of the Uzbek literary journal *Sharq yulduzi* (Star of the East).

Mr. Hashimov is the author of more than forty books published in Uzbek, Russian, and Bulgarian, among other languages, totaling more than two million copies in print. His work has been translated into Arabic, Czech, English, French, and Spanish. Mr. Hashimov is a State Prize Laureate and a National Writer of the Uzbek Republic.

Mr. Hashimov lives in Tashkent, where he writes and is editor-in-chief of *Sharq yulduzi*. The following selection is excerpted from his novel *Life in a Dream*.

W e were on board an Ilyushin 76. Just as they had packed the soldiers into the plane on the way there, coming back they crammed us together as well. The difference was that those going out had included my friends: Xayriddin, Temur (aka, Sasha) . . . The people around me now I barely knew. They were demobilized soldiers from various units. There was one other difference: We had gone out with luggage, but each soldier was returning with a single attaché case.

The roar of the engines was harsh to the ears. The young soldiers were silent. They were all thinking the same thing, but nobody dared to say it: "Let's just hope that a Stinger missile doesn't hit this plane!"

An unpleasant thought came to mind. I wonder if the "two-hundredth" load is on board? Probably not. They say that there is a special plane that carries back the dead bodies. The truth is, to those lying in the steel coffins, it's all the same. What difference does it make whether they bring them back on an airplane or whether they pass through Xayraton on a truck?

Fine, so your mother is pulling out her hair and wailing in grief. Your father, embracing the sealed coffin, is moaning, "My son, my dear child." The girl you love (if you have one), pressing to her face the picture you sent from "over there," cries silently through the night. How can she know if it's your body completely covered with blood lying in the box, or one of your boots, or just a bit of dirt?

The red warning light at the top of the cabin began to flash. Everyone looked instinctively in that direction. The door opened, and a pilot appeared.

"Boys, we've crossed the border!" he said smiling.

In a single moment the plane filled with a joyous uproar. While one wondered about the weather in Tashkent, another said he wanted to eat strawberries. A little farther down, one fellow, seated precariously on his attaché case, covered his face with his hands and wept . . .

The airport did not look like Tashkent's airport. (I learned later that we had landed at a different airport on the edge of town.) We entered a very narrow terminal. The suspicious customs officials began to inspect the soldiers' attaché cases as though each had smuggled in an atomic weapon from Afghanistan.

While I was standing to one side smoking a cigarette, I heard a very dear and precious song playing on the radio. I couldn't remember its name, but I wanted to cry.

As soon as I walked outside, a silver-white taxi sped up and stopped in front of me. The taxi driver, who looked older than he actually was, latched on to the attaché case in my hand.

"Where's your luggage, soldier?" he shouted.

He was surprised when I replied, "I don't have any bags."

"Get in! Hurry up! I'm not supposed to stop here. The State Inspectorate of Motor Vehicles will take my license away."

Who is this guy? I didn't call a cab!

"To the bus station!" I said, getting in beside him.

"Where do you actually live?"

"Far away. If you take me to the bus station, that'll be enough."

"Where do you live?" the driver persisted as he sped away quickly.

"In Piskent."

"Aren't we being funny! Even if it were all the way to Khotan I would take you there!"

"I don't have enough money to go there by taxi," I said, telling the truth. "If you take me to the bus station that will be fine."

"What does money have to do with this!" he gestured in

the air with his hand. "So to Piskent then?"

I quietly nodded yes, and then he asked, "Are you an Afghan vet? Come on, tell me, brother. So, in short, have you come back safe and sound? Your relatives' hearts must be about to burst from joy! As for me . . . I recognize Afghan vets from afar. I knew it immediately when I saw you, too. Don't rush off, I said to myself, let me help out this young fellow, I said."

Boy, does this driver talk a lot!

Tashkent had not changed. It was the very same city. The very same streets. Along the edges of the road bright green trees were blooming. Cars were chasing each other, blowing like the wind. It was as though the car ahead of us would not blow up when it hit a land mine. There were so many people on the street! So many decorations! Someone was carrying flowers? They were walking so freely and easily. It was as though the sniper hiding high in the rocks in the distance couldn't take out twenty of them in five minutes if he wanted to.

"Have you got any water fairy,* soldier?"

What is he saying?

"What?"

The taxi driver let out a big laugh.

"If I'm walking on branches, soldier, you're walking on leaves! What's your name?"

I told him.

"So, 'Rustamjon,' huh! What a liar!" As he was passing a police car on duty, he beeped his horn. "You're even wilier than I am! I noticed that your attaché case is light! But you can pack a lot of water fairy into one attaché case. One hit goes for five hundred rubles here! Did you hear, five hundred! If you say it's a deal, I'll pay you in cash! We'll divide it dry. Have we got a deal?"

"Keep your eyes on the road, brother!" I said gritting my teeth. "I don't have any water fairy whatsoever!"

---

*water fairy—slang for a type of narcotic.

"Is that so?"

The driver, believing me not in the least, looked me squarely in the face. "Last week I dropped a captain off in the Northeast area. We started talking just like this. What an excellent fellow he was! He seemed to be very open. He came back from Afghanistan with four suitcases, big ones. 'I'm an officer, I have no experience in such matters,' he said. 'If you can help me out, we can do business,' he said."

We left the city. Green fields began to appear. Along the side of the road were willow trees, and upright poplars were reaching to the sky. I noticed a familiar scent. At first I could not remember what it was. From where was the intoxicating fragrance coming? After going a kilometer, my eyes fell upon the silver-leaved *jiyda* off to the right, and my heart leapt. The *jiyda* is blossoming, the *jiyda*!

"Tell me the truth, brother!" said the taxi driver while speeding along. "Did you really not bring back anything from Afghanistan?"

"I did bring something!" I said, my patience wearing thin. "I brought back a pistol. It's in my bag."

Thank God! He stopped talking. The edge of the road was very green . . . Clover fields, cotton fields with the young plants newly emerging. Here and there sheep and spotted cows were grazing.

The driver stopped at the end of our street.

"Which house?" he asked loudly.

"Over there! It's the gate in the shadow of the willow tree."

"That's it! Get out!" He came around the car expressly to open my door. "First let them get their *suyunchi* * and I'll be off!" I stepped out.

By the time I had collected my senses, the taxi had already raised dust flying down the street to our gate, where it stopped. The taxi driver banged on the gate excit-

---

suyunchi—gifts given to the bearers of good news.

edly with both hands. In a flash he managed to let himself in. A moment later, he emerged with a new sheepskin coat on his shoulders and a new skullcap on his head. He motioned in my direction and said something. I saw my brother, Ilhom, standing in front of the gate, and I began to run with my heart racing. The taxi driver placed the attaché case at the foot of the willow tree and sped his car back in reverse. My brother also ran toward me.

When the car came up to me it slowed down for a second.

"Soldier!" said the taxi driver, sticking his head out the window. "Bless your brother for the three hundred he gave!"

I thought my heart was about to burst from my chest, and I ran involuntarily toward my house.

After embracing my brother, I hugged my mother, and she threw her arms around my neck. I realized with great heaviness that my mother had changed dramatically. Her scarf fell loosely to her shoulders, her hair had turned completely white, her arms were barely visible, thin as sticks. Tears streamed from her drawn and darkened eyes, and she kept saying "My child, my dear child" as she stroked my face.

I smelled the fragrance of basil, and my heart lifted. A precious, almost forgotten scent from my childhood . . . But why has her hair turned so white? It was not like that when I left! Why has her body become just a sliver? Is it possible that a human being can change so rapidly?

"Don't cry, Mother," I said laughing. "See, I've come back!"

My mother was still sobbing, hanging onto my neck.

"I'm not crying, my dear child," she said, wiping her tears. "You've returned, my dear child. After this I will never cry."

Strange, my older brother's wife also seemed to have aged a bit. As she kissed me on the forehead, happiness glistened in her tired eyes.

"That's enough, Mother," she said comforting my mother. "Thank God, dear Rustam has returned safe and sound. Now we have to have a wedding."

"Of course, we'll have a wedding!" My mother's smile alternated with her tears. "God willing, we'll speed up your wedding, dear Rustam."

As soon as I jumped across the threshold of the gate, my mother ordered my brother's wife excitedly:

"Salimaxon! Hurry up, dear child! Bring out the flatbread. Hurry!"

My brother's wife hesitated for a moment and then ran into the house. In a moment she carried out with both hands the flatbread with one edge bitten off. My mother handed it to me.

"Bite it saying, 'In the name of God,' my child!" she said, her voice trembling.

In my hands I held the flatbread that I had taken a bite out of exactly two years earlier on this threshold. My teethmarks were still visible on the flatbread's missing edge. A string was hung on one side of it. It's amazing that, having hung on the wall for two years, the bread had not gotten moldy; dust had not even settled on it.

"*Ilohi omi-in!**" My mother opened her sticklike hands in prayer. "May it be right that you have come home safe and sound, my child! May He make everything possible reach the intentions of His heart. May there be no war in this world or that world. May our Lord who created us protect us Himself from the perils of water, the perils of fire, and from the perils of slander."

The courtyard had not changed. Grapebuds were hanging from the grape arbor, which was attached to the roof of two of the first-floor rooms facing the courtyard. To the right was the bread oven in the corner, the open cattle shed with the crooked door; to the left my brother's

---

*Ilohi omi-in—literally, "May God let it be so."

44

thatched-roof house. All were exactly as they had been.

The two cherry trees near the low wall were bearing abundant fruit. (It was clear where the nephews and nieces had "damaged" the lower branches.) The apple tree by the shelter had shed its flowers, but its fruit was still small and difficult to pick out among the thick leaves. In the middle of the courtyard the Khokand roses that my father had brought with great excitement from Beshariq were budding. The rectangular flower garden was surrounded by a wire fence painted green. Basil completely covered the fence . . .

My brother's wife instantly made preparations under the arbor. She threw down layers of carpets and spread a tablecloth on the ground. My mother was seated carefully at the edge of the covered area and was again reading a long prayer. When my brother's wife thoroughly watered the courtyard, the scent of basil took over.

To tell the truth, I was hungry. While eating the bread fresh from the oven with a hearty appetite and drinking green tea, I thought that I had finally found the answer to the question that I had been turning over in my mind. Something was not right in the courtyard. There was usually a yellowish Niva car in the driveway with its top covered. My father practically never drove it; my older brother would drive it when going into the city or out to the countryside. Now the "garage" was cleanly swept, and there were no old canisters by the wall. Father must have gotten in and gone somewhere!

"Have you given my father the news yet?" I asked, gulping down my tea.

"We told him, my brother, we told him," said my older brother, slapping me on the back. "You just worry about that bread. You've probably missed Mother's bread! She's great, isn't she, Rustam! If she doesn't make the bread herself, she doesn't feel right about it. When I was going off to work this morning, she was kneading dough. If I say,

'Why bother, Salima will do it herself,' what do you think she says? Tell him yourself, Mother!"

My mother, looking first at my brother and then at me, smiled a bit, but remained silent.

"She said," said my brother in a festive voice, "she told me, you were saying, Mother, 'Ilhom, there will either be bad news from your brother today, or he will walk through the door himself; the dough foretold it, they say.' Isn't that so, Mother?"

"When I was dreaming . . ." said Mother, not taking her teary eyes from the tassels of the cloth on the ground. "It was a garden. A b-i-i-i-g garden . . . Then at one point a horse appeared in the garden. A snow-white horse. When I said, Oh, my child, when did you come? you laughed silently. When I looked, the horse had no reins. I got frightened. When I said, Get down, my child, get down quickly, it shouldn't run off letting you fall down, you still didn't say anything. Then your father appeared. When I said, Hey, Father, grab it, that horse over there, don't let it carry Rustam away . . ." My mother fell unexpectedly silent. She looked in the direction of the kitchen and cried out in a weak, sorrowful voice:

"Salimaxon-u-u! Hey, Salimaxon! You didn't give dear Rustam any yoghurt!"

My brother's wife peeked through the kitchen door.

"Run," my mother ordered her. "Go out to Aqida's. She should give us a bowl of yoghurt. Tell her that dear Rustam has come."

My brother's wife went out of the kitchen and raced into the street.

I was shocked.

"What happened to our cow?"

"May it die!" my mother shook her hand excitedly. "It stopped giving milk, we sold it."

"But there wás another one, too!" I said in amazement.

"We had that one slaughtered," my brother laughed

without paying attention. "Its stomach got bloated. I got caught up in the nephews' and nieces' play and didn't realize that it had wandered into the clover. Those naughty playful kids!"

To tell the truth, I was angry. How can one live in a village and not know how to look after a cow?

When my brother sensed what was going on inside me, he patted me on the back.

"So, brother! Why make such a big fuss? If your head is healthy, a skullcap can be found for it."

"Let me look after dinner while Salima is out," my mother said. Just as she was getting down from the arbor groaning, a happy voice was heard from the direction of the gate.

"Hur-ray, our uncle has come back!"

My brother's two sons raced into the courtyard. Speeding in like arrows, the two of them clung to me from two different directions. Both of them were drenched in sweat as though they had been playing soccer.

"What did you bring me?" asked the older one.

"What about for me?" asked the younger one.

"For you?" I asked rejoicing. "I brought you chewing gum."

A new commotion started:

"Give me ten pieces!"

"Give me fifteen pieces, okay?"

"He'll give you some. He'll give some to both of you," said my mother, shooing the children away from me. "Won't you go ask the neighbors for *suyunchi*? Won't you go tell them that your uncle has returned?"

The little nephews must have told the news to the whole village in an instant, because before the sun set we were flooded with guests. Tursunboy was the first to come. He began to lecture my mother as he embraced me and patted me on the back.

"Didn't I tell you, Aunt? Didn't I tell you that dear

Rustam would return without a scratch? As for you, you go around crying! Let's speed up the wedding, the wedding! I'll be best man myself!" He looked at me to confirm what he was saying. "Isn't it true, what I'm saying? Didn't I write that in my letter? There! One's word is true!"

A big place was set in the courtyard. Soup was prepared, the food was cooked.

I was starting to get angry that my father had not shown up yet. My brother calmed me down.

"There's a session going on in Tashkent. He'll be coming soon."

The guests left and the place became quiet. It was just the four of us again under the arbor at the foot of the apple tree. My mother, my brother, his wife, and I . . . It was who knows how late; the full moon affixed to the top of the willow tree opposite the gate was shining brightly, the locusts were happily singing.

It is bad that the moon is so bright. You can't even go piss at the gate. Protective gear covers your body. Under the cover of the rocks you are hidden from view, but you have a shadow, a shadow! Do you think that the "ghost" sniper lying in wait a kilometer away will not see your shadow? If he presses the trigger just once . . .

What is happening to me? Afghanistan is over! Far away in the distance! Behind cold mountains. Funny, why isn't my father here? What time is it getting to be? Can the meeting be taking this long?

"Brother, when is Father coming?" I asked, running out of patience.

"He's coming, brother, he's coming," said my brother energetically. "Sometimes a session drags on for three days. You know what it's like when one is a deputy . . ."

My nephew appeared in the entry in his underwear. The little one.

"Ow-w," he said, wanting to cry. "I need to pee-ee!"

My brother's wife ran to him. She led the child toward the bathroom. One could hear from that direction the words, "Be quick about it and go back to your place and sleep!"

My brother's wife was leading him back to bed when the child stopped opposite the flower garden. He turned to face the arbor and began to stomp on the ground and be capricious.

"Chewing gum! Uncle, chewing gum!" he said, about to cry.

"You little devil! I did promise you some chewing gum!" I jumped from the arbor and went into the entry. I opened the attaché case resting in the corner and took a pack of gum from among the toothbrush, towel, and other such articles.

"Here!" I said smiling. "A hundred pieces!"

"For me?" The little child's eyes opened wide with amazement, and he asked, "What about my brother?"

"There's plenty for your brother, too!" I said affectionately.

My brother's wife stroked the child's head.

"That's enough, go on. Go to sleep!"

Once I went back to the arbor and sat down, my little nephew appeared again. He ran up to us splashing in the area of the courtyard that had been wetted down. He was almost totally sleepless.

"Open it," he said, holding out the gum. "Open it for me, Un-cle!"

I sat the child on my knees and opened the gum wrapper. He chewed it with pleasure, drooling and smiling.

"Gee, Uncle, it tastes like strawberries!" He chewed it noisily for a while, and then hung onto my neck. "Un-cle!" he said, opening his deep black eyes wide. "You've come back?"

"You see that I'm back, don't you?" I said laughing.

"You're not leaving again?"

"No," I said amused. "I'm not leaving."

The little child thought for a moment and asked:

"Will grandfather be coming back from prison?"

It was as though something snapped inside me.

My older brother's wife ran up and slapped the child.

"Go on!" she said threateningly. "Are you going to die if you go to sleep, you little brat!"

"No-o-o! I'm going to sit with my uncle!" The child squealed, waving his arms and legs. "I won't sleep! I won't sleep!"

"Make him stop!" my older brother said sharply to his wife, gesturing angrily. "Take him inside!"

My mother began to rock and cry where she was sitting.

"God has dealt us a blow, my child! What sins have we committed against God, my son? Your poor father worked hard for so many years; is this what he's lived to see, dear Rustam?"

Translated from the Uzbek
by Uli Schamiloglu

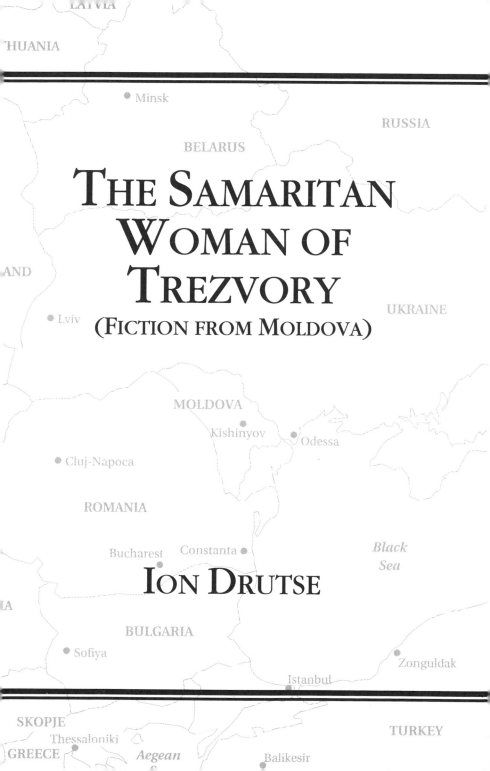

THE SAMARITAN WOMAN OF TREZVORY
(FICTION FROM MOLDOVA)

ION DRUTSE

Ion Drutse was born in 1928 in northern Moldova. He served in the Soviet Army and subsequently wrote for Moldovan newspapers and journals. In 1957, he was graduated from the Higher Literary Course. He is an author and playwright.

Mr. Drutse's first play, *Casa mare*, was performed in 1960 at the Central Academic Theater of the Soviet Army, traveled to more than 100 theaters, and continues in cinematic form to this day. After this followed five other plays that were performed at the Malyi Theater, the Central Academic Theater of the Soviet Army, and the Mayakovsky Theater.

Mr. Drutse is the author of several books. Three of his novels elicited heated controversy but were nonetheless published in the Soviet Union and abroad: *Vremya nashyei dobroty* (The Time of Our Kindness), *Zapakh speloi aivy* (The Smell of Ripe Quince), and *Belaya tserkov'* (White Church). The following selection is excerpted from his collection of short stories *Samarityanka* (The Samaritan Woman).

Mr. Drutse lives in Moscow.

In the fall of 1945, a government order to liquidate all monasteries came to Moldova. In the South they decided to start with the monks' monasteries, and in the North they chose the convents. Trezvory was the first to be closed. Early one morning the sacks of flour, bags and buckets, pillows and homespun runners, chickens and turkeys—all were loaded high and rapidly disappeared in four directions.

The speed and the well-organized manner in which this lawlessness was carried out left everyone paralyzed. Then came the hour when they actually started dismantling the churches and burning the sacred books. They drove out the animals and dragged out the church furnishings. The insolent gang, intoxicated not so much with the wine they had consumed, but with the sweet taste of destruction, were chasing after the young nuns. The horrified old nuns were crossing themselves and bidding each other their last farewells while they were shoved in groups into cars and driven away in different directions. In the middle of all this noise and confusion, a young girl of about seventeen approached the old, sick Abbess, who was standing there in despair. The girl quietly told the Abbess that the previous night she had seen an angel in a dream.

The word "angel" had a rousing effect on the old nun. She had been expecting a sign from God, or any kind of message from above, all day. She composed herself, comforted her flock as best she could, and found a quiet corner to talk to the girl.

"So what did he confide to you, my child?"

"He said: Leave your parents' house and go to be a nun."

"Nothing less than that! Your angel must think that it can be done in a day, or even in a morning!"

"And why not?"

"My child, you have to serve a novitiate for several years before you can take your vows . . ."

"Then take me as a novice."

"How can we take you? Don't you see that they are taking us away?"

"What should I do, then?"

"Pray to the Holy Virgin, thank her for the fair dream, and forget about it. You are young and pretty, the young men will soon be coming back from the war. Get married, have children, and forget about our grief."

"No," the girl said. "The angel told me to go to you and to live my life near the monastery springs, like that kind Samaritan woman who gave the Savior water to drink."

"Well," the Abbess said hesitantly, "the springs are over there, in the ravine. If you have time and desire, you can look after them . . ."

"But to be able to fulfill this task, I need someone to install me here. I need someone to order me very strictly what to do, and give me a coif, so that I can wear it like other nuns. Don't worry, I will wear it with honor and bring no disrepute upon your convent."

"Good Lord," the old woman said, "what do you need the bonnet for? Because of it they may take you for one of us, God forbid, throw you into a car and take you away."

"They won't. I had two brothers in the Army. One was killed, and the other came back. Please, give me a coif."

"But this is futility, my daughter!"

"I am asking not so much for my sake as for yours. If you allow me to wear the coif, you can go in peace. You will know that you did not leave the convent to the mercy of fate, that there is someone here who will always take care and preserve . . ."

"But to take care of what, my daughter? To preserve what?"

"Why, the churches. And the cemetery where many

deserving people lie. And then, there are the three springs."

"You are obsessed with those springs!"

"Well . . . It's not only that our convent got its name from the springs, but its very existence depended on them. I don't mean to hurt your feelings, but I believe that even after you are gone the water in the springs will remain cool, healing, and sacred . . ."

At this point, so the story goes, the Abbess embraced the girl, kissed her, took off her own coif, put it on the girl's head, and tied up the laces under her chin. Having done that, she seemed completely to regain her confidence. She found the officer in charge and announced that she and the remaining sisters would not leave the convent unless they were allowed to assemble in the main church to bid farewell to the altar and the bells. They say that her wish was granted, and that the girl was allowed to join them too, and that the Abbess kept her close the whole time.

Of course, legends are only legends, and some believe them and some don't. As time passed, some people who claimed to have exclusive information alleged that all this was old wives' tales. They were saying that when the convent was being liquidated, the girl came with others hoping to get hold of a pretty rug or something, but she came too late, when there was nothing left. All she found was an old dusty cap, so she put it on, and only after that came up with a story about her dream and the angel. They insisted that the girl could not possibly have met the Abbess, simply because the old woman was on the verge of losing her mind and was mouthing such curses that they took her away first, before dawn, even before the beginning of the operation.

The bells were silenced, the hotheads calmed down, and the dust settled on the road to the monastery. So was it good-bye Trezvory? Even though the nuns had been taken away and their property stolen, the monastery stood as it had before. Solid and elegant, it occupied a small plateau in the ravine, surrounded by hills covered with shrubs and oak trees. They had long since noticed that religious in general possessed a deep sense of beauty and understood its elevating power. The sites they chose for monasteries always were special places that seemed to bear a sign of Holy Grace.

From whichever direction one approached Trezvory, the monastery seemed a miracle born from the earth's depths and elevated in the palms of the mountains to be handed to the skies. From a distance, one could see the tall freshly painted white wall and the two clusters of green cupolas behind it. Inside, besides two cathedrals, were several large houses, some auxiliary buildings, and the long row of nuns' cells, which reminded one of a honeycomb.

All this was surrounded day and night with the light whisper of the springs, pleasant to the ear, chattering at the base of the rock on which the monastery stood. Actually, it had all started with the healing waters of those springs: According to legend, our founder and king, Stephen the Great, badly wounded in a lost battle, reached the springs one night. Since then, the fame of the springs spread by word of mouth as well as in written chronicles and schoolbooks.

I wonder: If it were up to you, dear reader, what would you install in this suddenly vacant place? A school? A hospital? A ranger's station? Well, maybe, but in Moldova they thought differently. Why, our wise heads asked, don't we put there a regional tractor maintenance yard, an MTS!* Of course, they had to overcome some obstacles. For example, how to get tracks up to the top of the mountain, when

---

MTS—Each machine tractor station served several collective farms in a given region. MTS's were expected to improve agricultural efficiency because mechanics, spare parts, and garages were all in one place.

there was not even a dirt road that a horse cart could manage? Or how to jam a garage and shops and all the offices into such à small space? Or, when the time came, how to get the thousands of tons of this tractor fleet down to the fields and later back up the mountain? As you can see, the problems were not small ones, but after all, isn't that what the people installed us for?

Done. Climbed up, wriggled through, and squeezed in. The more racket and mayhem, the better, so that the rest of the world will know that the new era has arrived . . .

A germ of destruction, perhaps, lies dormant in everybody, biding its time. So it was not extraordinary that the young men, recruited from the nearby villages to study in the tractor school, rushed into the vacuum to prove what they were made of. They created a whole new folklore: "true" stories of the intimate life of young nuns. Fiery imagination drove them on every evening as, walking home, they routinely stopped and wiped their tarry hands on the white monastery walls, leaving behind the kind of art and literature of which humankind has never been particularly proud.

To the disappointment of the would-be mechanics, their most brilliant comments would disappear before they had a chance to gain their rightful notoriety. The more colorful and witty the writing, the faster it was erased. It reached the point that the leader of the group had to stay on guard all night, and the censor was discovered. Ghostlike, carrying a bucket of whitewash, her white cap askew from her eager endeavor, a girl was busy nipping their wisdom in the bud.

"What do you think you are doing, you dope!" he demanded.

However, the dauber was not such a bad guy. He felt guilty for having frightened the girl, so he walked her home and even volunteered to carry her bucket. Near the girl's house, they sat for a while on a bench under the old chestnut tree. After some deliberation, the fellow asked for a glass of water.

It's an old tradition in Moldovan villages: If a guy likes a girl, he asks for a drink of water. The girl ran to the well and fetched a bucket of fresh water. After having two full mugs in gulps, the lad asked her the reason for her strange behavior. He would not leave off until she gave up and told him her story.

About a week later, the lad returned. Since she already had taken a vow and couldn't leave the monastery, he said, the logical thing for her to do was to marry him. After all, he said, it did not matter to him whom he married, so why not her? For her, however, there could be nothing but advantages: As his wife, she would be able to visit him openly in Trezvory and do there whatever she saw fit.

"And do you think we could actually move in there?"

"What do you mean, move in?"

"Well, let's say make a little house for ourselves somewhere in a corner?"

"Why not?"

They did not have a wedding feast: By that time the famine had started. They were married in a small church fifteen miles away where services were still held. After that, with the help of both their families, they put together a small hut in a nook right behind the main church. By Christmas, together with the first snow, a rumor spread in Northern Moldova that one nun was surviving in the Trezvory Monastery–tractor yard. In the daytime, one could see her, in a white coif, busily taking care of the grounds. In the evenings, as in the good old days, she walked down to the springs, and when she talked, her words were as clear and refreshing as the water of the springs itself . . .

Meanwhile, the MTS was gaining momentum. From morning to night, the engines wailed and the iron crashed.

The smart men were learning fast. They learned how to assemble and take apart a motor. They could start it, clean it, and tune it. They had even figured out where to get spare parts. The only thing they couldn't get right was the bean soup.

The problem was that in the drought year of 1945, along with the monastery liquidation campaign came the whirlwind of the compulsory meat and grain collections, sweeping through Moldovan villages. They took anything they could find. By winter, the famine came too. Half-abandoned villages seemed to be sunk in a kind of death-like daze, day or night. The MTS, however, was a new-era organization: It had no right to be torpid; it had to live a full-blooded life. The mechanics received a daily ration of bread, which most snuck home to their families. So the administrators determined instead to serve a hot meal once a day, and for that purpose brought a quantity of dry beans from the regional center every day, to make soup.

The beans started exhibiting some odd behavior right away. They shrank, slipped away, mysteriously disappeared, evaporated, and cooked down so much that when the hour arrived to serve the soup, there was not much there but clear water. Not a single tiny bean, not even a bean skin, not a vague resemblance of what used to be called bean soup.

"I wish they had left at least one nun here," the mechanics complained. "Ask the old people what great bean soup they used to make!"

"What about that young woman in a white cap?"

"Do you think we could actually accept her?"

"Why not?"

And that is how the good times came. Every day, at two in the afternoon, the thick smell of bean soup reigned over Trezvory. The only thing that bothered the mechanics was that the foolish woman did not squirrel away anything in her pockets and was always the last to sit down at the table. If there was anything left by that time, fine; if not, it was fine with her anyway. Even worse, however, was that she got it in her head that on the monastery grounds they should feed whoever was hungry. There was no telling how many hungry people were sneaking around every day!

The mechanics tried to explain to her that the MTS was atheist in character, but she threatened to quit the kitchen over such talk. They settled on the compromise that she could feed the strangers, but only with the leftovers. In those hungry years, however, leftovers hardly ever remained. On one gray spring day, she found a dying old man at the monastery wall and brought him to the table first, ordering him to sit there and wait. When he received the cherished bowl, the old man closed his eyes and breathed in the smell of the soup for long time. After it cooled, he ate it slowly. Then he stood, faced the empty right corner of the room where icons traditionally would have been kept, crossed himself, and pronounced in a suddenly strong voice:

"Thank you, Maika. I bow low to the ground and kiss your hands."

The thing is, in Moldova the name "Maika" is reserved for the most deserving and respected of nuns. And so it was that the rumor spread in the north of Moldova that even though the Trezvory Monastery had been liquidated and its churches stripped and services were no longer conducted, a nun still lived there. Not only could one often see her around the grounds, but they said that in time of trouble one could turn to her for help and be received, and fed, and consoled. As tradition had it, the nun would walk with you all the way down to the springs, sit with you there for a while, comfort you, and give you hope . . .

As time went on, somewhere in the mysterious depths of power the idea was born that MTS's had become obsolete.

The thing to do, they decided this time, was to give the machinery directly to the collective farms. So one fair day, after a long and painful occupation by the heavy machines, Trezvory Monastery became quiet and empty again. Two years passed while discussion on what to do with the grounds went on, with alternating intensity, on different levels. While they argued about it somewhere at the top, in the monastery two babies were born. The happy family was busy around the clock trying to bring the place back to life, so that the orchard and the vineyard and the churches would once again look like what are called orchards, vineyards, and churches in the rest of the world.

Now again I wonder: If it were up to you, dear reader, what would you place in such an abused and empty but still cozy and homey monastery? Maybe a museum of folk art? A research institute? A hospital for tuberculosis patients? I don't know. But in Moldova, no matter what seeds you plant, you can never be sure what you will harvest.

One day at dawn, the ravine, all the way from the river to the monastery, filled up with the roar of an exhausted herd. What stupid cowherd would drive his cattle into such a tight place? Maika thought. She ran out the gate, still half asleep. Couldn't he find a better watering-place? Meanwhile, the herdsman drove his cows higher and higher, and here he was ordering her to open the monastery gate. When Maika refused, he broke it open himself, and the cattle filled the yard.

As it turned out, the discussion had ended in the resolution to give Trezvory to *Zagotskot*, the regional meat supply station. The problem was, after the years of famine, the cattle requisitioned from the nearby villages were in such bad shape that the meat did not meet standards. The cows had to be fattened up a bit before transport to the slaughter-house. It occurred to somebody that Trezvory would be an ideal place for that. Certainly, there were some problems.

First, how to get the cattle there? They had collected some animals from as far as a hundred miles away. So what? Can't they walk? Second, how to feed the cows? No grass grows on these rocks, and the nearest train station is fifteen miles away. So what? We shall bring the feed over. That's it. That is what the people installed us for, to solve problems in a speedy manner.

She did not weep, or cry, or beat her head against the monastery wall. The main vow of a nun is to carry her cross humbly and obediently. So the former cook became a cow-woman. Together with her husband, from dawn to sunset, she chopped the straw, cleaned the stalls, hauled out manure, and carried buckets of water for the animals all the way from the bottom of the ravine. For more than three years, the thick stench of a cow shed reigned over the ancient walls and cupolas. The workers stole the grain meant for the livestock and forged the accounts of calves that allegedly fell off the rocks. For hours, they cooked the meat in huge boilers. The feasts were followed by endless drunken brawls. The murals on the walls in the churches grew moldy from the dampness, and the foundations of some structures sank. The constant traffic of cattle and machinery in the ravine resulted in the shifting of the natural soil layers, which in turn resulted in the disappearance of one of the springs somewhere underground. Who knows where all this would have ended, if not for that wonderful day when . . .

But no, the day was not really wonderful, neither for Moldova, nor for Uzbekistan, nor for the rest of the Union. History has its own way of intertwining events, however, and it is not up to us—witnessing only our own times—to interfere with the order of things. To make a long story short, a celebrated French writer, spoiled by fate and fame, visited Moscow with his wife and expressed a wish to visit the Uzbek capital Tashkent just on the eve of the horrible earthquake there.

Because of the catastrophe, they clearly had to change his itinerary, and someone came up with the idea of luring the famous guest to Moldova. After all, the capital city Kishinyov had been pushing for the title of "most hospitable city" for a long time. They prepared a reception on a most grandiose scale, but while on the plane there the celebrity happened to pick up a booklet prepared for foreign tourists traveling in the South. It is nobody's secret that our left hand often does not know what our right hand is doing. So it was no surprise that the cover was adorned by a picture of a curve of the River Dnestr, captured at sunset. In the background, glowing in the rays of the setting sun, the white walls of Trezvory Monastery stood in all their beauty, with two clusters of green cupolas behind them. The couple from the banks of the distant Seine were totally charmed.

"Would you like to go there?"

"Oui!"

The world knows that when a Frenchman gives his word to a woman, he becomes obsessed. What started then in Kishinyov! They exerted all kinds of influence and attempted all kinds of strategies. After one especially successful dinner with fine wines, they even attempted to fool the couple and send them in the wrong direction, but the writer turned out to have served as an officer during the war and had an excellent topographical sense. For two days the guests refused to leave their luxury suite in a hotel and even threatened to break off the visit . . .

At times you may actually believe that we are capable of working miracles. The authorities' call to save the monastery was answered by all the regions. People dropped their work in the fields and went to save the witness of their history. They cleaned, scrubbed, painted, and planted flowers—and when three days later a car with the important guests arrived, Trezvory Monastery stood in all its beauty. In the ravine the springs were babbling, and on the mountain serene sadness reigned, reminding a visitor of the imperfections of the world below. At the iron gate, repaired and freshly painted, a uniformed hotel doorkeeper with golden epaulets stood guard, as it is supposed to be in a civilized country . . .

Now, time passed and our people were not starving any more, dressed better, and moved into better homes. And the agonizing question, which always arrives on the heels of even relative prosperity, arose: What to do next? What had been the purpose of all the hard working, building, and accumulating? In other words, what does a person live for? What is life? For many centuries the church had taught that life is love. The aggressive side in a person is capable of destroying everything, and only love can create. Love is the medium, the only pasture in which the human spirit can ascend and thrive in the difficult journey to comprehend the eternal and the divine . . .

This is a disputable theory, perhaps, but the world has been standing on it for two thousand years and has not quite fallen apart. Having closed the temples and monasteries, the new order announced that life is nothing more than permanent class struggle and all the discussion about the soul is just useless talk. There is no spirit, only flesh, and there is nothing more to life than food and drink and sex . . .

Rumors that the final goal of Marxist teaching was the harmonious development of the human personality reached Moldova too. Nobody argued with that. Moldovans even tried to take steps toward this noble goal, but unfortunately people in our small republic couldn't stand any display of personality. For some reason mention of this mysterious phenomenon drove them mad, and they hurried to kill it in the bud, while it was still an embryo, a germ. Having accomplished that, the people of Kishinyov would assure you that they were prepared to go to any lengths and spare no effort to develop that harmonious thing. They just were not quite sure what it meant . . .

After having been liberated by the French humanist, Trezvory Monastery again fell into a time of uncertainty. Discussions about its fate continued at all levels. Remembering the embarrassment it had caused them last time, the republic authorities decided to protect themselves for the future and included Trezvory on the list of most valuable historic monuments. They even installed a plaque proclaiming that it was protected by the government. That plaque caused still more trouble though. The district administration was shocked that the republic administration took under its protection something that had escaped their authority. While this new argument was being resolved, the tireless family living in Trezvory found a bucket of green paint left behind by the workers who fixed the insides of the monastery and, ignoring all the safety regulations, climbed up and freshly painted all the cupolas. While the arguments continued, they dragged some white paint from somewhere and painted the outside walls as well. This accomplished, the Moldovan photographers wasted no time. Soon a series of excellent pictures of Trezvory found its way into the pages of the *Soviet Union**, to the horror of the local authorities.

Say, dear reader, what would you do now? What would you install in such an old but somehow indestructible dwelling? A summer camp? An environmental institution? A spa for collective farmers? I don't know. But in Moldova they had another urgent problem to deal with at that time.

At that juncture of Moldovan history it suddenly became clear that the Moldovans were lousy drinkers. They simply could not keep up with their brothers from other

---

Soviet Union—Soviet propaganda magazine published in foreign languages and distributed abroad.

republics. The pernicious habit of growing grapes in every yard, the hard labor from dawn to sunset, and the irregular nutrition eventually took their toll. En masse, people started getting intoxicated too fast. They would have just a drop of wine, in fact, just a smell of it, and there you were—they couldn't walk straight. Of course, when such an embarrassment happens in the bosom of the family, that's one thing. But what if there are strangers around, or even worse, important guests?

Important guests were coming to Moldova in droves at that time, by car, train, and plane, from all over the Soviet Union and even from some fraternal countries. A very important experiment was being staged there: industrial super-concentration and extra-mechanization. So it was vital to hide all these boozers as far away as possible. Of course, some uninhabited islands or deep thick woods might have taken care of the problem. In the absence of such, they decided to ditch them behind Trezvory's tall walls.

The former cook and cow-woman now became a nurse in a detox hospital for alcoholics. The methods of such institutions are well known: some emetic stuff mixed into a shot of vodka, plus the power of paternal exhortation. Concerning the exhortation sessions, the bums quickly learned how to shut them out. As for the rest of the treatment . . . Good Lord, that was Sodom and Gomorrah for you! Most of all, they suffered from the humiliation and the bitterness of their fall . . .

They were ashamed of their nurse and begged her not to come. Just stay home, keep yourself busy with knitting or spinning, make rugs or something, but don't come here. We will take care of everything ourselves. She smiled quietly, as if she were far away and neither saw nor heard them, and before they knew it she was back again. They cursed and damned her. It was not appropriate, they said, for a still young woman, who was raising two sons, to witness their disgrace and infamy, not to mention cleaning up after them! Even their families had abandoned them! But she only smiled at them from her never-never-land and came back again. She fed them, and cleaned up after them, and washed their clothes, and turned her eyes away only when it was really . . .

At late summer the prosperous life of our land reaches its zenith. On moonlit nights, when the scent of young fermenting wine breathes from every yard and they celebrate yet another wedding in the hills, the Trezvory prisoners, tormented by loneliness, lie two men to a bed in the main church, watching with glazed eyes a flying cherub in the cupola and waiting for their end. Life has no meaning for them any longer. However you look at it, everything is too late and senseless, but still death does not come . . .

But wait! The huge door opens quietly. A woman wearing a coif enters with two heavy milk-churns full of fresh spring water in her hands. The fact that she is the only one who has not gone to the wedding celebrations in the hills makes the poor souls feel that maybe God exists after all. And if that is so, perhaps it is worth taking at least one sip from the cool churn. Who knows, maybe the water in the springs is really sacred? In any case, a few sips of the water together with unhurried, kindhearted talk and some incredible intuition telling the woman at which bed she should linger and which could be left for now—all this helps to put together again the broken pieces of one more human fate.

Trezvory Hospital was regularly named the best in Moldova. Three years later, however the super-concentration and extra-mechanization campaign flopped, the tide of important visitors died out, and they decided to close some of the alcoholic treatment centers, Trezvory among them. The patients and personnel returned home, the equipment was moved to a nearby hospital, and all returned to normal: This one is to your health, and this one is to our health, and may you prosper, and may we prosper . . .

When a soul casts aside its path to God, human fate abandons its connection to the eternal source. Having lost that living thread—which starts with Adam and Eve, goes through our life, and disappears into infinite realms—we have limited our existence to the tiny space between two dates on a tombstone. This disappearance of the spiritual source of life opened the way to a materialistic orgy that to some degree drew all of us in. No wonder then, that our fates have fallen into the hands of all kinds of thieves and rascals. Endless "experiments" have left both the people and the land worn out, exhausted, and poisoned with pesticides. The rivers and forests are perishing. Together with wildlife, our people's star is in the descendant as well. It hurts to write about this, but out of every ten babies born in Moldova at least one . . .

Let me ask you again, dear reader, what would you do with such a divine place as Trezvory? Yes, you've guessed right this time. Indeed, they turned the monastery into a school for mentally retarded children. Of course, if we had islands or deep thick woods, we would have no problem, but we don't . . .

The cook, the cow-woman, and the nurse now became a laundress. The most amazing thing about her was this incredible mixture of will and determination with endless kindness and compliance. Her sons grew up, married, and moved away. One night her husband suddenly died. After his death, Maika asked someone to buy her a few yards of dark sateen, the kind they use for clothes lining. She made a cassock for herself, and covered her head with a dark cloth. Then she rolled up her sleeves again.

It was certainly very nice that the children of the school for the mentally retarded were all given jeans and denim jackets to wear. However, kids are kids, and denim is the hardest thing in the world to wash. Once soaked in water, it turns into wood. So it made two hundred pairs of wooden pants and two hundred wooden jackets, with wooden sleeves and metal buttons. All this had to be washed by hand and mended, and the rooms had to be cleaned too. After days of this work, the nights came, when the children cried, missing their families. Helpless in their anguish, these feeble children could not comfort themselves or each other. Instead, when one started crying, all the rest joined in. In the middle of the night, the heartbreaking chorus would awaken Maika. She would get up and go to this house of grief to console, and comfort, and once again to be somebody's mother, home, and hope . . .

One day, somewhere in Northern Moldova, I was wandering around a local cemetery, and came across Father Grigory, a priest whom I had known for many years. The old man was patiently waiting for the arrival of a funeral procession. It had been forbidden in Moldova for some time to have a priest openly accompany a funeral procession. For that reason, a priest would hold a small service in the house of the deceased and then a larger one at a cemetery, while the singing procession moved slowly along the village without a priest.

It was a hot day. We sat down to rest on a small bench near a grave. Our conversation was about those fifteen hundred churches and seventy monasteries that had been closed in Moldova.

"I think Zhabka Monastery is the only one left," Father Grigory sighed.

"Why, what about Trezvory?"

"There is a school there now for—what do you call them—idiots. There is also one spring left there . . ."

"What about the nun?"

"What nun?"

"Isn't it true that by a miracle there is still one nun there who survived?"

"Nonsense. That old woman was never properly veiled. She did not even receive the blessing to wear a cassock!"

Good Lord, I thought, what has happened to the world You created? Does not a whole life of kindness and mercy serve as sufficient evidence of one's devotion to You? Does one really need an official appointment? If Your servants understand Your teachings as words rather than deeds, aren't You afraid that Your churches may turn into just stages for the chorus, and the priests, in their gilded Byzantine robes, into fashion models?

Meanwhile, the years are passing, and one's fortitude is fading. Every spring older children graduate and leave, and new children arrive. Did you ever give a thought, dear reader, to where mentally retarded graduates go? Naturally, they go home, to their villages. Do you know how short is the life of these poor souls? Usually no longer than thirty, thirty-five years. They try to work like everybody else, but being truly invalids, they cannot stand up to the trials and hardships of healthy people. Neither can they drink as much as normal people, and sooner or later they get into trouble. The majority end up in prison.

Many of those who have done their time and survived don't know where to go. Often, they pass by their family houses and find themselves again knocking at the gate of Trezvory. They come back to complain of their fate, to get fed, cleaned, and consoled, and, maybe, to complete their life near the only one who loves and understands them.

"Thank you, Maika. I bow low to the ground and kiss your hands."

Translated from the Russian
by Sonia Melnikov

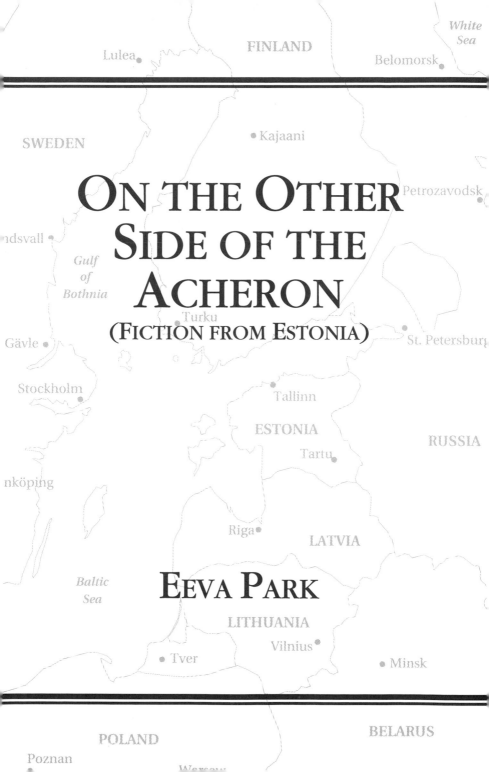

ON THE OTHER SIDE OF THE ACHERON
(FICTION FROM ESTONIA)

EEVA PARK

Eeva Park was born in Tallinn, Estonia, to a family with a long literary tradition. She began writing at an early age but at age sixteen, seeing that the young members of her family were all attempting to forge literary careers, she burned her stories and poems. Ms. Park was interested in history but was not allowed to study it at the university level because she did not join the Communist Youth League (Komsomol). She traveled extensively and pursued her creative impulse by painting on silk and porcelain.

Ms. Park is the author of two volumes of poetry, *Morkjas tull* (Acrid Wind) and *Oövalgus* (Light of the Night), a collection of short stories, *Hullu Hansu lugu* (The Story of Crazy Hans), and a novel, *Tolm ja tuul* (Dust and Wind). Several of her stories have appeared in the literary journal *Looming*. A collection of her short stories will be published imminently. Ms. Park was awarded the Friedebert Tuglas Prize for the best short story of 1993 for the following selection.

Ms. Park lives near Tallin. She is married and has three children.

The girl reached the street corner and turned toward home. She was dressed carelessly, yet in keeping with some principle of selection comprehensible only to herself. She was whistling. A melody from a Verdi opera haunted her. She whistled well, the tone pure and clear, and her body unconsciously followed the rhythm of the piece: Radames* arrives victorious. It was the greenest and warmest time of summer. The chill fog was gone from the nights. From one yard came the scent of newly mown grass. Catching that fragrance, she smiled; the whistle grew a shade louder and sounded across the small area of private houses. It was a day when everything made her laugh.

She had begun whistling while still in the center of the city. She had submitted her admission papers to the entrance committee and then walked, almost aimlessly, along streets covered with sun-softened asphalt. That day the light permeated everywhere, gilded everything. A damp wind blew from the sea, and at every ice cream stand long lines stood wilting in the heat. The girl couldn't bring herself to stop anywhere that long, not even for ice cream. She walked on and whistled quietly. The light pervaded everything. That day the drunkards staggering out of arcades were not from as different a world as they usually seemed to be. True, they stank more, but they did not keep to themselves as much. Overhead arched a securely blue sky, without even a hint of the dark infinity behind it. Sparrows hopped brazenly into the midst of a flock of pigeons and made off with a piece of white bread around which the entire flock had been fluttering. The girl laughed. The pigeons' wings, drooping on the dusty asphalt, gleamed iridescent green. Looking at them, the

---

*Radames—hero of Giuseppe Verdi's opera "Aida."

girl remembered someone's having told her that during the war German soldiers had caught and eaten pigeons. Picasso designed his party's symbol of them, plump, incapable of flight. Did he surmise something, or did he do it in dead earnest? wondered the girl, and that thought filled her anew with bubbling laughter. A woman who was passing by, dragging a child by the hand, misunderstood her laughter and responded with an angry sidelong glance. The little boy, his mouth smeared with dark jam, dropped a lard-filled pirogi from his hand to the ground, and the birds clustered around their new booty. They encircled mother and child, their hunger greater than their fear before human feet. The boy tried to pounce on their tails, but his mother pulled him along forcefully.

"Stop that!" she said and swatted the back of his head with her pocketbook. The boy let out a screech. His hooting was audible far off, but not a single passerby even glanced in their direction, and that too amused the girl.

And there, on the front lawn of the Artists' House, stood a bronze bust. It was Estonian wrestling champion Georg Lurich, looking as if he had sunk into the ground up to his chest. His countenance was smooth and self-possessed; he reflected back light and coolness. The girl wanted to rest her cheek against his, to cool herself, but she saw her bus approaching the stop and she had to go.

On her own street, she slowed her pace. The street was quiet and empty. Where her fence began stood an unfamiliar Russian Volga with all four doors thrown open. Along that hushed street the sound of footsteps carried far; the girl was still whistling, but mechanically. Coming abreast of the car, she nearly stopped. Inside sat four strapping, taciturn men. They did not look at each other or at the girl, either. They were all similar in some way, dressed alike, almost as if in uniform. On any other day their noiseless sitting would have had, if not a frightening, at least a threatening effect on the girl. Now, however, she burst out laughing. The scene was reminiscent of a bad low-budget film, it was so incredible and yet true. None of the men turned his head when she passed; the echo of her footsteps did not appear to reach their ears. It seemed to the girl that the four of them actually looked alike, and none seemed tormented by the heat. All were wearing jackets. There wasn't a trickle of sweat visible—their faces weren't even flushed—and each sat as if he were alone in the car. At the last moment, the girl felt an impulse to step over to the car and ask for something stupid, like tea or water, a glass of water. That would have sounded especially good in Russian, *stakanchik vadoo*, but when she cast a glance back over her shoulder, she met the gaze of the man behind the steering wheel and she lost the desire to say anything. The gaze was so listlessly apathetic, vacant, sunk into the ground like Lurich's legs on the lawn in the city. The girl reached her gate, looked at the windows of the house inquisitively and back at the car once more, then she went into the house. The guests had long since arrived. The smell of coffee and sandwiches drifted into the vestibule along with loud conversation in Finnish. Her mother came through on the way to the kitchen and, meeting her daughter, said:

"So here you are! When you're needed, there's never hide nor hair of you to be found. Just like an alley cat . . . And just look at you. For goodness sake, put on something else before you go say hello . . . And that hair, you really have cut it ridiculously . . . I just don't have the energy to deal with you."

"I was hoping that they'd already split . . . Don't get excited, I'll sit quietly in my own room."

"Are you crazy? I already said that you were coming. You go greet them politely, and don't embarrass me. Go right this minute!"

Her mother stood firmly blocking the corridor, and the

girl, seeing the narrow line into which her mother's lips were pressed, stepped through the doorway and into the largest room in the apartment. ·

The light filtering into the room through the pine branches gave it the greenish tinge of an aquarium. There were almost twenty guests from Finland; it looked as if they were already feeling good. At the girl's greeting, their conversation subsided for a moment, but soon the difficult-to-follow jumble of conversation was rekindled. An extra table had been brought into the room, as had all the chairs in the house. Initially it seemed that there wasn't a single place to sit. The girl decided that she would just say her obligatory hello, take a look around, and leave; but when she had studied the guests for a moment, she zigzagged over to the windows, pushed open one that was ajar, and waved a festive greeting outside. Seeing that she was being observed, she said in Finnish:

"You are very important guests! We've never before had the honor of being so openly under surveillance."

"Who? What?" came a confusion of questions.

Her mother had appeared at the door, and from there she looked at her daughter with shocked reproach. When the girl pointed out the Volga behind the fence, everyone crowded to the windows and peered briefly at the gray car and the four silent men visible through a sparse, stunted lilac bush.

"What kind of talk is this?" said the mother. "You'll frighten our guests away."

"They're sitting here so wide-eyed and cheerful, and they think they really aren't so far from home at all, just across the Gulf. I wanted to show them that they've come across the Acheron*. . . Besides, rest assured, they like this. It's exciting, almost romantic," the girl said in Estonian.

---

*Acheron (ak' uh ron)—in classical mythology, one of the five rivers of the underworld, which separate the world of the living from the world of the dead.

"Sit," said the mother, "sit over in the corner behind the desk . . . I've got enough worries even without you."

The mother smiled a sparkling, light, conquering smile at the guests. She passed pastries and poured fresh, hot coffee into all the cups that weren't completely full. Excusing herself, the girl climbed over the legs of a young local poet and sat down in the indicated corner. From there the immobile car was barely visible behind the greenery in the yard, and the girl was a bit ashamed of the scene she had caused. The young poet seemed just as uncomfortable as the girl. Either he didn't know Finnish or he felt himself to have mistakenly strayed into the city during the summer heat, but he remained silently morose and, peasantlike, a long straight shock of hair hung over his eyes.

The conversation, which had gone slightly awry with looking at the car, rose again to its previous brisk level. A lot of open bottles stood on the table. One younger Finn appeared to be reaching his limit. Every time the girl raised her clean-shaven head, she saw the man's slightly misty glance. The girl and the young poet sat motionless for a long time and were silent in accord.

The girl smiled; her good mood was beginning to return.

Everything was too bizarre to be taken seriously for long. Sitting on her uncomfortable stool, she stretched, and her foot slid forward, striking something. Looking under the table, she saw a flat whiskey bottle hidden there. Jostling her neighbor slightly, the girl ducked halfway beneath the desk, and when she sat up again she nudged him with her shoulder and said softly:

"Look what I found."

The poet nodded with almost ceremonial gravity and pushed his unruly hair, which kept falling forward, behind his ear. Now he looked even more like an Indian chief who had lost, found, and then lost a tribe again. The girl unscrewed the cap and poured whiskey into both their coffee cups, which no one had remembered to fill. She put the bottle back under the table with a swift motion, this time right beside her foot.

"Whose health shall we drink to?" she asked. "Those around the tables, or those outside?"

"Let's drink to our own health," answered the poet.

The girl had never drunk whiskey before; it went down so quickly and searingly that she gasped for air. The poet pressed a sandwich into her hand, and the girl gratefully bit off a large mouthful. Silently, and in accord as before, they drained the bottle. It went so quickly that they didn't even have a chance to get drunk before it was all gone. Just then the mother brought out to the table the crowning glory of her immense preparations for the reception, a whipped cream torte. The girl laughed, looking at the white heap. Her mother had never been a great cook, but that torte, bulging over the sides of the platter, had completely lost its shape. Bits of chocolate bristled chaotically in every direction, and the berries appeared to have been thrown into the whipped cream in a fit of anger. When it came time to lift pieces of it onto plates, the girl suddenly noticed a foul odor from the john predicting a change in the weather.

"Smell that?" she said to the poet. "Reality's pressing in, the weather's starting to turn. Take a whiff!"

They sniffed together.

"I thought that was from the torte," said the poet. "I thought it didn't sit well with the whiskey."

They had a long laugh.

"It does. But only if you're sitting in the john," said the girl.

They laughed again.

"This is serious," said the poet.

"The *smell* is serious," said the girl, and this time they were totally unable to stop laughing.

"Now there are two possibilities; no, three," said the girl, drawing a breath. "Either we all sit like this, as if there weren't any smell at all, you know, polite, educated, proper people . . ."

". . . and famous," said the poet.

"And famous. Or I dash out of here and open the window of our disgraceful john . . . but when I open the door a strong whiff is going to come in here. In the midst of the whipped cream. And the wretchedness of our life will be apparent to everyone."

She looked gravely at the poet, who looked at her sadly in return, and then they both burst into laughter.

"What's happened to you two over there? What's making you so gleeful?" asked her mother, and suddenly both the girl and the poet realized that everyone was looking at them. They hadn't even noticed when they had become the center of attention.

"Oh, never mind us," said the poet and pushed the shock of hair back from his eyes. "Just glad to be alive, that's about the size of it."

The girl sank against the bookshelf with laughter.

The room seemed even more like an aquarium than when she had entered.

It was already late afternoon. Green light filtered through the pine branches, and the gray Volga stood just at the last fence post, its doors open and, inside, four glum men.

Translated from the Estonian
by Ritva Poom

THE GUESTS
(FICTION FROM TURKMENISTAN)

ATAGELDI GARAYEV

Atageldi Garayev was born in 1943 in Karabekaul *etrap* (county), Turkmenistan, three months after his father went to war. As a result, he was named Atageldi, which means, in Turkmen, "Father returned." His father did in fact return. Mr. Garayev studied at the Pedagogical Institute at Trebzoy, where he received a degree in history. In 1984 he was graduated from the Moscow Higher Literary Course. He has worked as a journalist and departmental director at various newspapers and magazines, including the literary magazine *Garagum* (Black Sand), and as an editor at a publishing house. He is a member of the Turkmen Writers Union.

Mr. Garayev is the author of a number of books. He has published articles, stories for children, and novels. His work has been published in Czech, English, Estonian, French, German, Russian, Spanish, Turkmen, and other languages. The following short story is excerpted from a cycle of four short stories entitled *When Camels Fly*.

Mr. Garayev is married and has two daughters and two sons.

*D*uring the Soviet period, Turkmenistan was forcibly converted from a pastoral, oasis-oriented society to an agricultural monoculture, namely cotton. This has had disastrous long-term results. The Turkmen Steppe, most of the country, is riddled with poorly built irrigation ditches and pumping stations equipped with antiquated machinery. The soil and the water of the Amu Darya have been contaminated with chemical fertilizers. Public awareness of the consequences of this and other ecological problems triggered Turkmenistan's first dissent in the 1980s.

After the collapse of the Soviet Union, Turkmenistan's ruling Communist Party changed its name but not its methods. All press media are controlled by the state, and protest is suppressed.

The anecdote at the beginning of the following narrative is one of the countless stories attributed to the medieval "wise-fool" of the Turks, here called Ependi.

Once Ependi, in a bad mood, stepped outside with a friend, and a crow that had been circling overhead landed on the roof of his black house. Ependi burst out laughing. His friend looked at him in astonishment and said:

"Ependi, why are you laughing? You came out of the house in a bad mood, and now?"

At that, Ependi pointed at the crow and said, "It is just that I like the fact that birds fly and camels cannot. If camels could fly, it would be horrible. If *they* landed on a building, they would smash it to pieces."

Ah, Ependi, Ependi, how wonderful must have been the time in which you lived, the Middle Ages! In those days, flying creatures flew, and flightless ones did not. But now, the flightless beings fly faster and farther than the flying ones.

You don't believe me? Look! Look! When a camel flies, it spreads its wings and soars into the sky. If only you could hear the sound of its wings! *Swish! Swish! Swish!*

It makes a noise when it takes flight, and drops of white spittle fall from its mouth onto the faces of workers, peasants, and honest people. They are afraid of sinking into this white foam. As for the camels, they take pleasure in human misery, they gloat over human misfortune. When the camels trample through the sky, thunder rumbles and lightning strikes.

Men drink, they huddle together, they get demoted, they gather into crowds, they step all over each other. As for the camels, they fly, they eat and drink what men have earned, and gloat over it, then spit in men's faces.

Now and then, one of the camels alights on a house and huddles up on it like an orphan. The house trembles and then crumbles beneath its weight. Imploring voices can be heard from beneath the rubble. The voices of the people cry out to the heavens for help, but no help comes because camels are circling, their flapping wings making a horrendous racket above all the houses. They cannot be driven away or shot down because they are exploiting a special right, namely, that they have the right to everything and others have the right to nothing. If someone doesn't want the camels to destroy his house, then he must do as the camels say. He must give the camels his finest foods, while he himself eats thorns and weeds. He must fall to his knees and say, "I am boundlessly grateful for this great happiness." Otherwise, the camels will reduce his house to ashes. If they destroy hundreds of houses it is nothing. If they drive hundreds of people into madhouses it is few. They need many things, many, many things! When camels fly, it is horrible, quite horrible! Do not cut the wool of camels, cut their wings, their wings!

Otherwise, hang yourself by a rope from your roof or you will grow terribly thin from cancer of the esophagus and will die covered with cancerous boils.

*   *   *

But pardon me, I do not mean to frighten you or show you that life is lousy. I am more or less telling you the truth: I am saying that when camels fly, things can get very bad. I am demonstrating the burden I have taken on myself.

I work like a slave, but you're not aware of this. Maybe it's for the better. Working long days, forgetting the world, and when I don't feel well, what a pleasure it is to take a rest. I have little time to notice camels. No, that's not true; it's impossible not to notice them. They can follow you into your soul.

Now my mother can't sleep, there's an uproar on both sides, she feels a bad day is coming to her only child. But there is nothing she can do about it.

When camels fly, one can never rest comfortably.

*   *   *

I did not set out to write an ode of praise. Like Jelaletdin, I wanted to tell the truth. I wanted to yell out, "People, do not be indifferent, take a look around you. We are aboard Noah's ark, and it is leaking. If we don't plug the leak, we will drown!" That's why I collected my camping gear and some food, took a vacation from work, and returned to the woods.

I must be frank: By day, this place is pleasant, but at night, frightening. Jackals howl, and wild boars grunt . . . And one could die from mosquito bites. When mosquitoes from the countryside land on you, they usually look for a soft spot in which to sink their scalpels. Here the mosquitoes come at you like dive bombers.

My first night here, jackals ate the meat I had put in the pot.

My misery increased when I discovered that the water of the Amu Darya, once sweet as honey, had become painfully polluted, and then mixed with the salty and poisonous waters of the irrigation canals. The river tossed and turned like a sleeping mother worried about her children. It bubbled away muddily. Not staying in its bed, it overflowed angrily.

I pitched my tent under a tall willow tree where cows were chewing their cuds, bulls were butting each other, donkeys were stamping, and all of them were flicking flies. There was a herd of horses on the other side of the river. An antiquated irrigation pump was rattling away. I intended to write a story.

It wasn't coming. The needed words were as cagy as fish, and the unneeded yammered in my head from every direction like the speech of a chairman at an important meeting.

The words drilled into my head like a centipede and got stuck between my skull and my brain. I could not shake them. There was no place I could go to escape their absurdity. They consumed my brain like a boll weevil eating its way through cotton and turned my brain to straw.

I held my head in my hands, regretting a thousand times my ever having come to this place. I stood up and cried out, "What's wrong with writing at home!"

While I was pacing back and forth, crushing everything in my path, drowning in these thoughts, I heard a car. The sun was just sinking below the tops of the trees.

The car bulled itself through the underbrush and stopped. One of the two men who got out was the chairman of the regional industrial organization, or *raypo*; the other was a leading car salesman, Jeppi, the *raypo's* first cousin who ran the automotive dealership.

"What are you doing here?" they asked. I looked at them curiously.

"It's tiring to write in the daytime," one of them said to the other, "and impossible at night. If he's not yet a great poet, he is still a poet from our country." Then to me: "If we're disturbing you, say so, and we'll go."

If only I had been able to write one line. "I've been writing so much, my arms are tired," I lied. "It's nice that you came."

"How much do they pay you per word?" asked Jeppi, staring at the paper in the typewriter. It was difficult to answer the question.

"Ah, whatever . . ." I said, shrugging vaguely.

"There is nothing anyone would pay for here," said the *raypo*. "This is the tail wagging the dog. If I spent my time doing this, I would have thousands of *manat** in my wallet. But he is still young and spreading it a bit thick." He stroked his potbelly. It struck me that he was like a small child, showing off his belly, and I smiled.

"One shouldn't make a lot of money. Money is the enemy of humankind," said Jeppi, who had been standing there quietly. I had grown up with Jeppi.

"Do you know this for a fact?"

"Yes." Jeppi's voice sounded hoarse.

Kadir, the *raypo*, waited to hear what I would say.

"Those who write spend their lives gossiping about businessmen," he finally stated.

"It's not gossip; it's the way they are," I blurted out.

"You're malicious, boy! You are no Seydi—a poet who could draw a sword and mount a horse." Kadir's eyes were angry when he said this, but his lips were smiling.

"But then," he continued, "from what I've heard, our writers don't have to be angels. As they say, whether the wolf eats or not, he has blood in his mouth. Those who are considered writers have more dirt on their hands than we do. They wallow in it, but the mud they sling sticks to us!"

I didn't know what to say, so for a long time I was silent.

"Ah ha . . . the writer is silent," said Kadir.

"First, I'm not a writer; second, time will tell what will stick to whom."

"Yeah, listen to that, he says time will tell," he said. Jeppi began to smile. Kadir had offended me, and I thought I would get angry. I was very insulted.

"Don't feel insulted about your writing. Time will tell

*manat—currency of Turkmenistan.

what kind of talent you have. We didn't come here to argue with a poet from our own region. We came to meet, sit together, become friends. We didn't mean to draw blood."

"If chickens have any blood," said Jeppi. He patted Kadir's massive stomach. I was surprised at their words.

"Is there a chicken here?"

They looked at each other and laughed.

"If we could get us a pheasant it would be good."

I wondered what they were trying to pull.

"It's forbidden to shoot pheasants!" I said.

"You don't have to tell us, we already know. I've read a lot of novels in the newspapers with titles like 'We Must Protect the Pheasants,'" Kadir said, and laughed at me. He called articles "novels." What he said was one thing, what he did another.

"You can't shoot pheasants," I stated categorically. "I would make you something to eat, but the jackals ate my food last night."

Jeppi burst out laughing, "My little brother the writer has had quite a day."

Kadir took a pull from a bottle, looked at Jeppi and asked, "What are you laughing at? . . . As long as there are incompetent hunters like you, foxes and jackals have to make off with the weekly earnings of the only writer working in our region. Go get the glasses from the car."

Jeppi went to the car with a lightness that did not befit his body.

Kadir, like the tempters of old, wanted me to drink some vodka. I said that I couldn't drink vodka, that my body had a bad reaction to it. He said, "In my entire life I never met a writer who didn't drink." Later, though, he realized that I was serious.

"Well, okay, if you don't drink, then don't drink," he said. Without wiping off the neck of the bottle, he took a large slug, then peeled a big onion and threw it into his mouth. He wiped his gold teeth. "Either drink, or shoot us a pheasant."

"Shooting a pheasant is better than drinking vodka." I picked up my rifle and stood up.

"And writer, don't waste time. I'd hate to think you're a person who hesitates and is lost. Go! Go!"

Look, I write a lot of articles arguing that "We Must Protect the Pheasants." I've criticized some people and demanded that action be taken against others. If *I* shoot a pheasant, they'll take pleasure in it. They don't need pheasant meat or pheasant soup; they only need for me to shoot a pheasant. I recognized their crafty plans, but for some reason couldn't come up with one of my own.

. . . I went to the bank of the Amu Darya. I washed my hands and face in its filthy water and listened to the pheasants squawking. The sun set suddenly, and their sounds ceased.

Cutting through the dry underbrush, I entered the sparse willow grove. I saw a pheasant hanging off a branch. I fired a shot into the air, and the pheasant fell from the branch. It had apparently been dead for a while. I skinned it, removed the claws and head, and washed it in the river.

"I have it."

"You really left us in an agony of suspense, but no harm done. But where's its skin, its head, and legs?" Kadir asked. He looked at the pheasant in my hands with pleasure.

"I cleaned it in the river."

"Look at that, when the writer does something, he does it right. And if the dogs don't know, the dogs don't bark. Jeppi, see if you can cook this hen."

"You're my guests: I shot the pheasant myself, and I'll cook it myself," I said. I did not want Jeppi to get near the pheasant, so I hurried to start the fire.

I lit the kindling, sprinkled tamarisk in the pheasant's cavity, and put it on the fire. While the pheasant was cooking, they talked about the openmindedness of writers.

Jeppi had once lost his wallet in Ashgabat and inquired at the Address Bureau where the house of a well-known writer was. Without even knowing him, the writer had given him twenty-five *manat* and cheered him up.

"Ach, you're talking small change. There are writers who have given their *lives* for the people. Didn't you ever hear of a Tatar writer named Musa Jelil?"

I immediately corrected him: "Musa Jelil was a poet."

"If he writes, we call him a writer," said Kadir, and continued, "Musa Jelil was such a hero that he captured five German generals."

Jeppi opened his mouth to say something. I stood up in order to control my rage. I asked, "Kadir, what institute did you graduate from?"

"The Institute of Trade."

"Then don't talk about things like Musa Jelil; talk about business."

"You're belittling us because you're the ruler of this realm. Whatever you say, that's the way it is."

"Will you allow us to drink?"

Kadir, without waiting for me to answer, got two bottles of vodka. The two men shoved meat into their mouths. Jeppi took another drink and another bite. "There's a smell of carrion about this," he said and frowned.

"If it were up to the jackals, pheasant would stink like carrion," said Kadir, laughing. I joined in his laughter and, very slowly, inched toward the underbrush where the rifle was. Jeppi downed two glasses of vodka, one after the other.

"You're the only writer in the village, our pride and joy, so don't take what we say here to heart," Kadir said. "You've pleased us, and we're satisfied with you. Whenever you need anything from the black market, just ask. Now, we'll get going. It's getting late. We'll come again tomorrow: Save a couple of pheasants for us, and we'll give you a hand."

"Everyone should have some land," said Jeppi, his greed

for land confounding his hearing. He poured another glass of vodka and, throwing back his head, drank it down without a blink. He reached for the pheasant, tore off another piece, opened his mouth wide, shoved it in, and began to chew. Suddenly it struck him that I was not eating.

"My brother, you are not eating," he said, and stared at me, chewing.

"You are my guests, eat up! There are lots of pheasants here. Later I will shoot another one and eat it." Jeppi gaped at me, and I began to look at him slyly. Jeppi opened his jaws wide as he chewed, chewing the meat a long time, grinding away and grinding away, and finally shut his eyes and swallowed it.

The writer seizes the opportunity to slip away from Kadir and Jeppi as they continue to indulge in their feast. Realizing that he has disappeared, they go after him. While being pursued, the writer muses on the decline of Turkmen society: It has become more concerned with money than with common human values. Kadir and Jeppi catch the writer and, although he threatens them with his rifle, they know that he will never shoot. They bring him down from the tree in whose branches he was hiding, beat him up as a warning of what will happen if he informs the newspaper about their confessed black market activities, tie him to a tree, and depart.

All of a sudden, he remembers high school graduation night.

"You are a young man graduating from a Soviet high school who has received the education of a Soviet society," said the tall, brown-faced director of the school. He was called the "Spirit of Aghayunus" among the students; he smiled and displayed beautiful white teeth. "And you are an active member of our Komsomol* . . . Tell us how you feel."

There was a long pause.

---

*Komsomol—Communist Youth League. Party organization for young adults (14- to 28-year olds).

"We had things crammed into our brains for several years. We entered and graduated from high schools successfully at the cost of money earned by our mothers and fathers. We are capable of increasing the yield of milk, butter, meat, and eggs collected from every cow . . ." But before I could finish, Spirit of Aghayunus' face grew dark and the whites of his eyes grew large.

"Does a cow lay *eggs*?" the director asked, menacingly. There was laughter in the lecture hall.

"When students who cannot properly write their own names or the names of their fathers graduate with a certificate of honor, isn't it the case that cows lay eggs?" I asked.

"You are a slanderer!" spat the permanently red-faced mathematics teacher, poking me with his finger. "Because you didn't receive a certificate of honor, you hurl slander at others."

Perhaps because I had studied my history lessons well, or perhaps just generally, my history teacher Jelaletdin liked me. He couldn't bear the anger he saw on my face. He suddenly rose to his feet.

"Uh, in the history of the school, in the history of the whole society . . . ," he began to gasp for breath: It was as if he couldn't utter the words he wanted to say. He stretched out his arms and stood there. Then: "Look, are there any students who can answer the mathematical questions on the state examination? No! Can you, the mathematics teacher, do them yourself? No! Can *any* of the mathematicians in the school do them? No! But if someone drives a big car and gives you a sheep, do you not arrange to have his children transferred to a better school?" he asked and clenched his fist.

"Slander!" cried the mathematics teacher, making a zero with his fingers, and again, "Slander!" drawing a big zero in the air with his hands. "If you add zero to zero, it is zero," he said, and sounded as if he were drowning. "If you add slander to slander, it is pure slander."

"You say it's slander, but I'll prove it. A person doesn't need the sword of Goroglu* for that—I can do it myself." Jelaletdin went on the offensive. "When I was only a youth of seventeen, I brought Fieldmarshal Paulus to his knees. And you, what did you do?"

"You could not have brought Paulus to his knees, not even if you begged him."

"Every era has its own weapons," said Jelaletdin, waving a fist in the air.

"You can't . . . " sputtered the physical education teacher. "You should be ashamed of saying such things in front of the students!"

"These aren't students any more. They're grown up, and it's time they learned the truth." These words were directed at the physical education teacher, who bore the honorary title 'Little Tree of the City Soviet.'

Trembling with rage, Jelaletdin continued:

"I 'can't'? . . . I should be 'ashamed'? Why should I be ashamed? It is you, you who should be ashamed! You should be ashamed of cheating them up to now. I always told the students the truth. Let the bosses hate me, abhor me for this, let the leaders throw me to the dogs, but I always told the truth and I always tell the truth!"

Then he began to speak in a very low voice. "Once they wanted to accept a candidate into the Party. One of the Party examiners asked him, 'Who is the secretary-general of the UN?' The unfortunate one stood there mute, not knowing the answer. One of the other examiners whispered almost inaudibly, 'U Thant, U Thant,' because U Thant from Burma headed the UN. The candidate shrugged his shoulders and gasped as if he had been struck. Turning crimson with anger at the question that had been put to him and having misunderstood what was meant as a helpful whisper, he yelled, 'What do you mean, I can't, I can't? Why? Why should I be ashamed? *You*

---

*Goroglu—epic hero of the Middle Ages.

should be ashamed—you said you would get me into the Party. You are the one who took a thousand rubles from me! I took nothing from you! You should be ashamed!'"

Then Jelaletdin turned and said, "Comrade director, why should I be ashamed? You should be ashamed. You! You try to look good in front of the leaders, but you sent the students out into the cotton fields to help with the harvest instead of into the classrooms; you turned a blind eye to this. You should be ashamed!"

The director did not get angry. Instead, he smiled and said, "As for what you say, I cannot say that it is untrue. But come now, let us agree that 'The friendly devil is better than the useless angel.' Let's give the students a chance to dance and sing. Strike up the music!"

Warm music began to resound. He said, "Get everyone in the mood; I will take care of the rest." My fellow students began to dance and whirl in circles. I was not in the mood to celebrate.

In front of my eyes whirled 'calving chickens' and 'egg-laying cows' gorging themselves on twenty to thirty kilograms of feed and fifty kilograms of hay a day, and sheep dying of starvation.

Translated from the Turkmen
by David Nissman

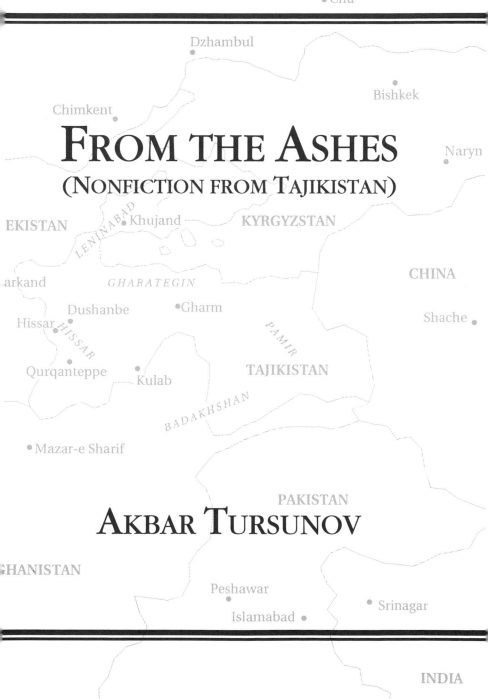

KAZAKHSTAN

Chu

Dzhambul

Bishkek

Chimkent

FROM THE ASHES
(NONFICTION FROM TAJIKISTAN)

Naryn

EKISTAN   Khujand   KYRGYZSTAN

LENINABAD

arkand   *GHARATEGIN*   CHINA

Dushanbe   •Gharm   Shache

Hissar   *HISSAR*   PAMIR

Qurqanteppe   Kulab   TAJIKISTAN

BADAKHSHAN

• Mazar-e Sharif

PAKISTAN

AKBAR TURSUNOV

;HANISTAN

Peshawar

Srinagar

Islamabad •

INDIA

Akbar Tursunov was born in Isfara, Tajikistan, in 1946. He holds a doctorate from the Institute of Philosophy, USSR Academy of Sciences in Moscow. Dr. Tursunov was a corresponding member of the Russian Academy of Sciences and from 1986 to 1993 was director of the Institute of Oriental Studies in Tajikistan. Dr. Tursunov was one of six individuals chosen to act as peace mediators between the Communist government of Tajikistan and the anti-Communist Opposition in May 1992.

Dr. Tursunov is a senior researcher at the Center for Strategic Research, a branch of the Institute of World Economy and International Relations in Dushanbe. He has published approximately fifty articles in Tajik and Russian journals and newspapers and is the author of several books.

Dr. Tursunov, who is currently a visiting scholar at the University of Pennsylvania, lives in Dushanbe. He is married and has one daughter and three sons.

My eyes dried today, for crying over yesterday,
Alas, which eye will cry tonight over my tomorrow?
—Akhavan Sales

The twentieth century has witnessed its share of bloody social revolutions in Europe and Asia. Each time, revolutionaries declared war on the ancient institutions which, they claimed, had fostered the poverty, and they promised to lay the foundation for a palace of happiness. But although the majority of revolutions have succeeded, none has achieved its goal: The ancient institutions have been turned into ashes, but no palaces of hope or monuments to happiness appear on the horizon. At best, some bleak, ephemeral buildings remain.

Each time, intellectuals furthered the call to revolution and heralded its advance; each time, ironically, they themselves became the first sacrifices at the altar of revolution—see the workings of time and tide! Ream after ream, the cherished writings of those innocent souls were turned to ashes, along with their bodies and dreams. It is, it seems, an element of human nature to gather any pieces that may have survived and mastermind yet another revolution.

Perhaps the most pretentious of world revolutions was the October Revolution of 1917 in Russia. Espousing an all-knowing and all-embracing ideology, the Bolsheviks aspired to place themselves at the forefront of world communism. What followed was an intense barrage of Communist propaganda that persuaded people, even the educated and civilized, that the new union was the epitome of human social progress. This notion of social progress gave rise to Stalin's "Progressive Socialism," and that in turn underlay Brezhnev's "Ideal Future Society." The world was expected to view this progress with envy and imitate it with a longing heart. Perhaps the lesson to be learned is that the Soviet people themselves believed in the system. They believed that the "Soviet Order" was just, trustworthy, wise, pure, and sincere. Otherwise, why would generations have endeavored to destroy the foundations of tyrannical capitalism to establish communism? Why would generations have destined themselves for doom?

Then change occurred and altered our ways. Six years of Mikhail Gorbachev's program of *perestroika* and *glasnost* (1985–1991) opened our eyes not only to see our past but to be ashamed of it. So much for a "shining future"!

At the beginning of the twentieth century, Mirza Sirraj, one of the wise and learned sons of Tajikistan, traveled to Europe. Upon his return, this enlightened and patriotic man published an interesting travelogue. Strolling along the clean and beautiful avenues of Paris and recalling his impoverished country and ignorant compatriots, the Tajik traveler and thinker pondered, "Observe to what heights science and wealth have elevated the Europeans and to what depths our illiteracy and laziness have reduced us, the people of Asia. Observe their expansive horizons in life and our limitations and servility. When the Prophet spoke of cleanliness as an article of faith, whom did he have in mind? We, too, are human beings . . . We, too, have desire . . . for prosperous cities with beautiful buildings. Pity us . . . Pity . . . "

Reading these lines from *Tuhaf-i Ahl-i Bukhara*, I am filled with sorrow. The tomorrow that our intellectuals anticipated with such zeal at the beginning of the century has not yet dawned by the close of the century. What has made the difference?

During their long history, the Tajiks have experienced a number of assaults on their national identity, so much so that European historians have wondered at the resiliency of their ancestors. "How have these people," they marvel, "survived the triple calamity of the Mongols (thirteenth century), Tamerlane (fourteenth century), and Shiban Khan and his descendants (sixteenth century on)?" Compared to those attacks, the tsarist Russian takeover of the fifteenth century was the least dangerous; but in the process of colonialization, the Russian tsar killed so many that scales cannot measure their loss. The heir to the tsarist regime, the Soviet Union, lasted for just a lifetime. But during those seventy years it committed atrocities the likes of which the Tajiks' seven-hundred-year history had not previously witnessed. In seventy years, our language all but vanished, and our culture was severed from its roots. The Russians altered everything from the alphabet— which was changed from Arabic to Cyrillic—to the calendar. We were separated from neighbors who shared our Russian language and culture, Iran and the Tajik minority in Afghanistan, as if by the Great Wall of China. Our country was transformed into merely a source of raw materials, our diverse agriculture was reduced to cotton and tobacco monocultures, our land was destroyed, and our environment poisoned. The damage to our rural areas cannot be recompensed.

However, let us not be thankless. The Tajiks did not stagnate for seventy years. They did try to lift themselves up by their bootstraps. Unfortunately, when the future of the former Soviet republics was being decided, their luck ran out. At that moment, those who lacked all gained all, and the Tajiks, who had everything, lost everything.

That statement may sound like a riddle, but it is really quite simple. I am referring to the fact that in 1924, Moscow established the national-administrative divisions that determined the territorial rights of the peoples of Soviet Central Asia.

It began with Stalin's politically motivated decision to

divide and thus weaken the region of Turkistan. Moscow recognized Uzbekistan, Kyrgyzstan, Kazakhstan, and Turkmenistan as republics. Tajikistan, however, was initially classified as an autonomous republic under the auspices of Uzbekistan and only later as an independent republic. The national-administrative divisions of 1924 reduced Tajik territory, reassigning much of Tajikistan's most valuable land to Uzbekistan. As a result, 93 percent of the new republic, "Red Tajikistan," was mountainous, and 75 percent of its inhabitants were farmers. The new divisions allowed the Uzbeks to keep the cities of Samarkand and Bukhara, Tajikistan's ancient cultural centers, leaving the Tajiks stripped of their historic centers of cosmopolitan trade, intellectual life, and civilization.

The Tajiks were further isolated by Moscow-approved programs meant to impose Turkic and Uzbek—as opposed to Iranian—culture. Further, the Moscow-led policy of Sovietization severed Tajiks from their culture and their sources of spiritual inspiration. At the core of Sovietization was the elimination of traditional moral and intellectual values. Tajiks were prevented from maintaining cultural ties with the neighboring Iranians and Afghan Tajiks and thus denied access to their ancient Iranian roots. Instead a semi-European culture, filtered though Soviet culture, was imposed. Over the years, without the benefit of their intellectuals, teachers, economists, and politicians—most of whom had been forced by economic necessity and Soviet policy to remain in Samarkand and Bukhara—the Tajiks failed at nation building. They fell prey to economic, social, and educational decline. Their very world view was affected.

Whether by accident or by divine decree, stagnant Soviet society was shaken by Gorbachev's *perestroika* or, shall we say, *catastrophka*. The slow but steady change in the Union eventually reached our quiet corner and awakened its inner forces. What happened thereafter was not only beyond Gorbachev's control but beyond the imagination of the Soviet Union's most ardent enemies. The inevitably declining Soviet superpower allowed its constituent republics to thumb their noses at the KGB and the Communist Party and dare to break away and, one by one, declare political independence. For many, the joy of independence was soon to be marred, however, because they did not know the first word about independence. Tajikistan is a case in point; any Tajik intellectual will tell you that there can be no political independence without economic freedom.

Today, all the former republics are in dire straits; and among the Muslim republics the situation in Tajikistan borders on desperation. Seven decades of Russian centralized control over the economy devastated it to the point that, short of large infusions of foreign aid, it will not recover. Long-term Russian control over science, technology, and education drained the republic of its independent scientific and technological talent. There are no textbooks written by Tajiks; the current instructional materials are all translated from Russian and reflect none of the experiences of the Iranian peoples or of Muslims in general. Discussions of those peoples' advances in the economic, social, scientific, and educational spheres are routinely ignored. Actors, artists, authors, and educators alike lack studios and schools. In the shattered economy, denied the employment of their God-given talents for the elevation of their condition, Tajiks walk the streets of Dushanbe, Khujand, and Kulab aimlessly. Some have joined the new business world, but their lack of capital, experience, and expertise prevents them performing their business honestly. People openly shirk their responsibility and refuse to discharge their duty. A kind of demoralization has set in that is neither spiritual nor psychological. The question to be asked is this: How did all this come about? What is the history of this demoralization and degeneration?

The Communist Party of the Soviet Union endeavored to create a melting pot consisting of nationalities, cultures, and languages that had little or nothing in common. Out of this experiment was to emerge the "new Soviet man," an individual endowed with the highest ideals of the Communist hierarchy. Had the experiment worked, the new Soviet man would have encompassed the best of humanity's ethical and spiritual values, been at one with his society and endowed with the ethical purity that the ancient Iranians expected of their best. But the "Soviet man" that emerged was insensitive to and extremely inconsiderate of the pain and suffering of society. He was socially and politically active, but his energies were directed to only one end—that of his personal elevation. Rather than promoting ethics, he made traditional values, ethics included, subservient to his own whims.

In Tajikistan the result of the imposition of this new Soviet culture was the appearance of a bevy of pretender scholars and opportunistic politicians whose hunger for respect, wealth, and power could not be sated. (After the collapse of the USSR, the greed of these self-identified "intellectuals," their grab for power, and their lack of savvy in the workings of democracy combined to promote neo-communism, chaos, and, ultimately, civil war: It was their slogans and their barbarous and murderous acts that incited the ordinary Tajik to take up arms against his fellow citizen.)

There were also upright and brave individuals, true intellectuals, individuals whose moral compass was not influenced by ephemeral political considerations. I personally know a number of scholars who bore the brunt of Stalin's wrath but did not change their philosophical ideas. I know poets and writers who, despite the directives of the Communist regime, refused to lend their pen to empty praise of the system. They preferred to maintain the eternal integrity of their thousand-year-old cultural heritage. But they are in the minority. What can be said about the majority of the intellectuals of the Soviet period is that they chose to go along with the tyrannical regime not because of a weakness of personality but because of the tragic situation in which they found themselves; they mortgaged their souls to the devil to find respite for their bodies. They had to make sure that they followed Communist ideology according to the guidelines established by political overseers, for seventy years the sole authorities on science and culture.

With the downfall of the USSR, the oppressive state structures gradually became obsolete. And even though, chameleon-like, many citizens superficially changed color to deal with the realities of a market economy, it is no surprise that at the deepest level they had not changed. After all, communism, Bolshevism, fascism, and the like promote particular deeply held world views. Does not each of those -isms bring about a culture of its own, a culture that smacks of Manichaean pessimism, violence, and bigotry?

For seventy years, Bolshevism was imposed on Soviet society. It has deep roots not only in our spiritual world but in our very psyche. Just as an image is etched in granite, so the rules of Soviet political behavior were indelibly engraved in the conscious and subconscious of every heir to the Soviet legacy. Communism as a superpower has left the scene, but its belligerent ideology, like a radioactive dump, continues to poison our environment.

In the last few years this post-Soviet culture, soaked in partisan politics, has dragged Tajikistan into turmoil. Political parties and movements with democratic platforms have sprung into existence at the drop of a hat and have disappeared as suddenly. The reason is that they all sprang from the same old Russian mold and were ready to commit the same crimes, even murder, if such actions brought them closer to the achievement of their political goals. Recent events in Tajikistan testify to the fact that the real aim of these parties and movements has been to destroy the republic's constitutional government. Using diverse political dodges, upstart groups in Tajikistan attempted to impose themselves on the populace and failed. Their individual failure gave rise to the formation of an alliance, the united Opposition. The clash between the Opposition and the government developed in three phases and led to civil war.

Phase I. On November 20, 1991, presidential elections were held and Rahman Nabiyev was elected president. But from January until May, 1992, the Opposition pressured and derailed the elected government. A coalition government, known as the government of national reconciliation, was formed, with Opposition leaders having a share of power. The Opposition declared its cooperation with President Nabiyev.

Phase II. Despite its promises to contribute to the strength of the nation and government, between June and September the Opposition followed its own hidden agenda. It intended to rule at all costs. The Opposition leadership undermined the president. Before long, Nabiyev's rule became crippled, domestically and internationally. His economic, social, and political programs remained unrealized. The Opposition tried to cajole Nabiyev into resigning voluntarily. He refused. The President was forced to resign at gun point.

Phase III. Over the course of the next three months, the impending calamity finally struck. Armed members of the Opposition, supported by the Dushanbe mafia, assumed control of the capital city, Dushanbe, the region of Gorno-Badakhshan, and the Gharategin Valley. Two other major regions, Kulab in the south and Leninabad in the north, refused to recognize this government. They formed a Popular Front and began to resist militarily the brutal attacks of the new government in the south with the

The Battle for the Tajik Constitution

The struggle between Communists and Muslims for control of Tajikistan dates back to the 1970s and 1980s, when sporadic anti-Communist demonstrations were held. After 1982, the Tajik leadership suppressed Islamic activities in some Islamic regions. These undemocratic measures led to the dismissal of First Party Secretary Rahman Nabiyev by Gorbachev in 1985.

Gaining strength, in 1988 the Islamic community chose Tajikistan's first Islamic chief judge and expanded its influence into the villages. In 1989 a change in the language law made knowledge of Tajiki necessary. This and the specter of Islamic rule frightened non-Muslim citizens living in Tajikistan, many of whom left for Moscow and elsewhere.

Following the dissolution of the USSR, the struggle over the Tajik constitution heated up. On one side, pro-Communists wanted to retain the Soviet-imposed constitution until a new constitution could be forged. On the other were those Muslims who wanted to adopt *Shari'a*, literal execution of Islamic law. There was also a third group, anti-Communists who wanted a new constitution but a secular one.

On February 12, 1990, the first major confrontation between Muslims and Communists occurred in Dushanbe. A number of people were killed or wounded. That year, the Democratic Party of Tajikistan—a secular, Western-oriented party—was formed. Simultaneously, the Resurgence Islamic Party (IRP), which sought to introduce *Shari'a*, was legalized after fifteen years of clandestine activity.

By early 1991, a strong anti-Communist opposition had developed. The IRP, the Democratic Party, and several Islamic groups from different regions contended individually for control of Tajikistan. When that failed, they agreed to overlook their differences and formed a united front, the Opposition. They forced President Nabiyev to hold a presidential election. In November, Nabiyev won the election. His ally, Safarali Kinjayev, became Chairman of the Supreme Soviet.

On March 25, 1992, Kinjayev publicly accused Muhammedayaz Novjavanov, Minister of the Interior from the Pamir region, of embezzlement and of overstepping his authority. Novjavanov resigned. The next day, some 300 Pamiris gathered in front of the Central Committee headquarters to protest the humiliation of their compatriot. They demanded Kinjayev's resignation. Nabiyev ignored the crowd, which increased daily.

In mid-April, Islamic Chief Judge Akbar Turajanzada, his followers, and other Opposition adherents joined the demonstration. Originally a Pamiri protest, it now became an Opposition protest. On April 22, Nabiyev made concessions to the crowd: Kinjayev was replaced by a Pamiri, Akbarshah Iskandarov, and half the seats in Parliament and eight important government posts were yielded to the predominantly Islamic Opposition.

Days later, demonstrators from Kulab and Leninabad, traditional Communist strongholds, gathered in front of the Supreme Soviet building to protest the newly reconfigured government. As a result the Opposition crowd returned. Tensions mounted.

On April 29, encouraged by the support of the Kulabis and Leninabadis, Nabiyev reinstated Kinjayev. Two days later, he secretly organized an anti-Opposition force, the Popular Front. On May 5, he armed its members.

This sudden reversal of presidential policy and an accidental shoot-out in front of the National Security Committee building ignited the tinderbox of Communist-Opposition tensions throughout Tajikistan. A massacre occurred on May 5-10. Prominent Communist leaders fled Dushanbe. Before long, the south was engulfed in civil war. The Popular Front fought Opposition forces in the south while Nabiyev and Kinjayev fought the Opposition politicians in the Supreme Soviet in Dushanbe.

The Supreme Soviet, after a vote of no confidence, forced Nabiyev to accept a coalition government. Control of the government now passed to the Opposition. The Opposition continued the war in the south against the Popular Front throughout the summer.

On September 7, the Opposition forced Nabiyev to resign at gunpoint. Iskandarov became Acting President. The 201st division of the Russian Army, stationed in Dushanbe for years, now took control of the city and seized former Soviet industrial complexes as Russian property.

On October 24-25, after failing to restore the government to Communist rule by force, Kinjayev persuaded the Russians to set a date for a meeting of the Supreme Soviet at which the fate of the nation could be decided. Accordingly, on November 16-19, the meeting was held in Communist-controlled Khujand. Two Communists were elected Chairman of the Supreme Soviet and Prime Minister, respectively.

In early December, Dushanbe was "readied" for the arrival of the new government. The Popular Front, Russian troops, and troops from neighboring Uzbekistan—all of whom had their own political and economic reasons for wanting to prevent the Opposition from ruling Tajikistan—converged on Dushanbe. The Opposition and those associated with it were liquidated. Dushanbe was reportedly full of corpses.

The leaders of the Opposition fled the country.

—Iraj Bashiri

ultimate goal of overthrowing that government. This gave rise to civil war. In the end the Opposition was defeated by the Popular Front.

But while some intellectuals grabbed for power after the dissolution of the Soviet Union, others, myself included, joined together to plan for the modernization of Tajikistan. This group of enlightened progressives is dedicated to bringing Tajikistan into the twentieth century where it can stand shoulder to shoulder with other nations. Rather than simply imitating the models at hand, we seek to forge a new model that synthesizes the best of foreign ideas with Tajik national traditions and culture. Our contribution to the creation of the coalition government, our efforts to make that government work, and our efforts to negotiate an end to the civil war were all focused on the realization of that sublime goal. There were, however, forces in society that could not be overcome. We were overwhelmed by a public that lacked political awareness and was inexperienced in the formation of democratic institutions. Most of all, we were defeated by religious bigotry and infighting between different regions of Tajikistan. We failed because we could not muster the knowledge required to run an independent state in the late twentieth century. And in that sense we, the intellectuals, are to blame for the onslaught.

Today, the majority of the ruling elite are former Communists and members of the militia who are still devoted to the defunct ideology of the past. They are not well disposed to science and culture and are not likely to promote them. All the professors, poets, authors, and journalists of note who cooperated with the Opposition left the republic, along with their leaders, after the current government seized power. Most of the intellectuals who chose to stay or who had no alternative but to stay were arrested or deprived of their livelihood. They are constantly harassed by the government-run media as to where they were and what they were doing during those fateful days.

The future is dim, even dark. The new rulers may not state their claim openly; but they, too, patronize the few remaining scientists, authors, and poets only in order to promote themselves. This dim prognosis leaves me no alternative but to foresee a stalemate in our scientific and cultural affairs for many years to come. Now that Soviet dominance has been lifted, we will ultimately confront the same reality that our Iranian brothers confronted in the 1970s—we will have to struggle to bring about an independent nation that is no longer under the sway of a dominant foreign culture, in this case, Communism. And we will have to pull ourselves out. But note this difference: The Iranian intellectuals whose concerted effort liberated their country from foreign dominance were graduates of American and European institutions. They could easily travel abroad. Can we do the same with only Russian?

Translated from the Tajiki
by Iraj Bashiri

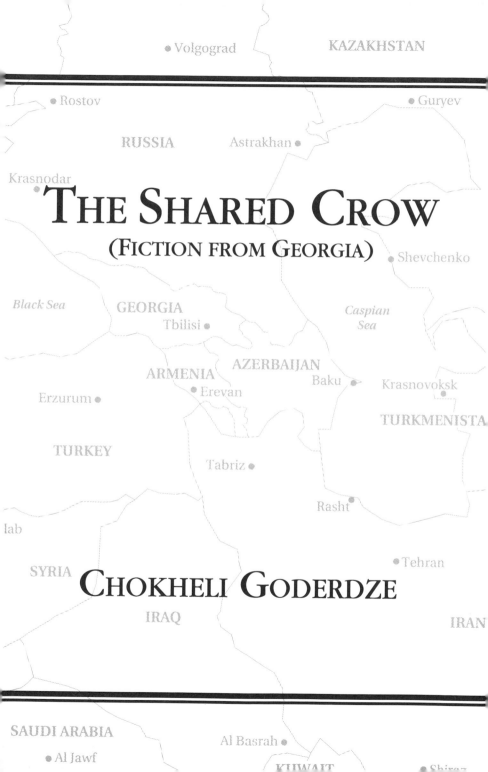

THE SHARED CROW
(FICTION FROM GEORGIA)

CHOKHELI GODERDZE

Chokheli Goderdze was born in 1954 in the village of Chokhi, Georgia. In 1979 he was graduated from the Film School at the Tbilisi State Theater Institute. He is a writer and filmmaker.

After graduating, Mr. Goderdze worked as a director-producer at GeorgiaFilm Studios. He has written and directed ten feature-length and short films. In 1982, he was awarded the Grand Prize at the Oberhausen International Film Festival and two Silver Nymph prizes at the Monte Carlo International Film Festival.

Mr. Goderdze is the author of three novels and a collection of short stories. When a volume of his stories was published in Russian, it was named Outstanding First Book. His stories have been translated into several languages.

Mr. Goderdze works at GeorgiaFilm Studios in Tbilisi. He is married and has two children, Nika and Luka.

W*hile still a Soviet republic, Georgia had within its boundaries two autonomous republics, Abkhazia and Adjara, and one independent department, South Ossetia. Many have argued that Stalin formed these political enclaves less for the benefit of ethnic minorities than to weaken any independence movement that might someday arise: If three or four nationalities coexist within one nation, how is nationalism defined? If so, the savage fighting in Abkhazia and Ossetia following Georgia's declaration of independence on April 9, 1991, is evidence of just how potent his strategy was. Moreover, it has been suggested by some that Russian intervention and provocation set Georgian against Georgian, helping spark the civil war in 1992 that pitted elected President Zviad Gamsakhurdia and his forces against the pro-democracy forces led by Eduard Shevardnadze. The war ended with Gamsakhurdia's suicide in 1994.*

With so many struggles for power, land, and sovereignty, it is perhaps not surprising that people have dug in and fought for every last inch of what they consider theirs — and that many have been forced to eat crow.

"Last name?"

"Chokeli."

"First name?"

"Butula . . ."

"Occupation?"

"The village priest."

"Whom are you suing?"

"Makhara (Ghkvtisavar) Shughliashvili."

"On what grounds?"

"Because they claimed my crow as their own, reformed her, and now insist she is theirs."

"How now your crow? Are you trying to make a fool of me?"

"The whole world knew that the crow was mine. She would follow me everywhere, to the fields and the meadows . . . She was mine, and now they have won her over."

"Wait, wait . . . So you say you had your own crow, right? . . . And what might be the name of your crow?"

"Um . . . of the crow?"

"Yes, the crow."

"Nothing. People called her 'Butula's crow'."

"So you didn't call her anything . . . I see."

"What do you see?"

"I see that you yourself have misappropriated the crow."

"As God is my witness . . . I . . ."

"God?! Don't start with your 'God' nonsense!"

"Forgive me . . . I just . . ."

"Citizen Butula, how long was the crow in your possession?"

"Nine years, Your Honor."

"And why don't they let you have her back?"

"They insist she's theirs."

"Whom does the crow wish to stay with?"

"They've deceived her, Your Honor, they feed her day and night. And so she now flies to them all the time."

"They don't call her by a name either?"

"No . . ."

Butula and the judge discussed the issue of the crow deep into the night. The village priest left the court so exhausted he was hardly able to ride his horse home.

"So?! What did he tell you? Will we get paid for the crow? . . . Come on, speak up!" insisted Butula's wife.

"He said that both of us are guilty! That first I adopted the crow illegally and then Makhara did, all with some dark, hidden intentions."

"And what about the money?"

"The money? We may yet be fined a hundred rubles."

"Why?!"

"He said that tomorrow morning he'll come to our village

and test our story. I will have to put food on one side of the porch, and Makhara on the other. We'll have to stand by our own food, while he stands in the middle. We will wait for the crow and see what the crow does. If she flies to my food, Makhara will have to pay the hundred ruble fine, but if she flies to Makhara's food, then I'm stuck with the fine."

"Are you crazy? We had barely a hundred rubles in donations at the last holiday, and now you say we might have to pay all of that out in fines. Don't you know she'll fly to their side?"

"That's what he said. What am I to do?"

Next morning the entire village congregated around Shughliashvili's porch. On one side of the porch stood Makhara and on the other, Butula. In the middle of it all stood the gloating judge.

Half of the village sided with Butula, while the other half sided with Makhara. But the final say in the matter would be the crow's.

The wait for the crow was a long one. For some reason she was late. The judge even suspected he was being made a fool of, but every time he looked at the distressed faces of Butula and Makhara, his hope reemerged. In fact, he would become angry with himself for not having set the fine at two hundred rubles.

Suddenly the crowd stirred. The crow had appeared in the sky and was circling the clouds, slowly coming down upon them. While awaiting the bird, Butula and Makhara almost fainted.

At last the crow descended, flapped her wings, sat on the judge's hat, let out a loud caw, relieved herself, and flew away.

Makhara and Butula were elated, figuring they had just avoided the fine. But the judge wasn't giving up so easily; he quickly regained his senses and set forth a new accusation upon Makhara and Butula.

"Considering that you illegally adopted the crow for some dark, hidden reasons, didn't give her a name, and furthermore have morally depraved her, each of you is now obliged to pay a fine in the amount of two hundred rubles; otherwise criminal proceedings will be held against you. You have one week to make full payment of your fines."

The judge cleaned his hat, put it on, and left.

Makhara was fretting over how to come up with two hundred rubles. Butula, though, had a glimmer of hope: At the last holiday the congregation's donations to the church totaled a hundred rubles, and there was another holiday coming up in two days.

Unfortunately not all that many people came to the church for the holiday, and Butula couldn't equal last holiday's donations. Makhara wasn't able to come up with the money either—everyone who knew what the money was for refused to help him. They would slam the door in his face, muttering, "Go stare at the crows, maybe they'll throw you some money."

At week's end the judge summoned both of them and held them in custody.

Each day witnesses were summoned from their village, to learn the identity of the crow. Some avoided repeated interrogations by bribing the judge at the very first meeting. Upon returning to the village they would brag about their clever behavior, especially to those who had already been questioned eight times.

The whole village was distressed. They collected four hundred rubles to take to the judge to bail out their co-villagers.

The judge tapped on the table and threw the money into the table drawer with such a dissatisfied look on his face that the leaders of the village lost hope.

"I will grant your request only upon the condition that

you catch that crow and bring her here, alive, personally to me!"

The entire village, young and old, searched for the crow, but she was avoiding everyone now. She would come to the village only rarely, perch on a branch, caw for a bit, and fly away. They couldn't catch her, and they didn't want to kill her. The judge wanted the crow alive, and they feared that a dead crow would bring them even harsher punishment.

At last an idea dawned upon Gamikharda:

"There is no way the judge will be able to recognize the crow by her face."

"Sure, he won't remember."

"Then let's catch another crow and bring it to him."

"Good idea."

"And what if he does remember?"

"How can he possibly remember the crow's face after having seen her just once? Even then I doubt he got a good look. She sat right on his hat, did her business, and flew away."

"But what if Butula and Makhara turn us in? What if they tell the judge it's another crow? . . . What then?"

"Let's send somebody to notify them of our plan so that they will keep their mouths shut."

And so they sent someone to warn Butula and Makhara.

In the orchard an old crow had her nest. She always raised her offspring there, and the villagers had become so accustomed to her that they never bothered her. She also realized the benevolence of the people and never stole a chick from anybody's yard.

The people had no choice. They decided this was the crow to take to the judge. They sent the children up the tree to bring her down.

Poor crow: She so trusted the people's kindness that she

gave no resistance at all.

As the men carried her, the women wailed with pity for the crow:

"Your poor luckless children!"

"Oh, goodness, they are orphans now!"

"And poor us! We are even worse off than they are. They say a crow lives three hundred years; by then the judge might die and she'll be set free."

"Not three hundred, but rather sixty."

"No, woman, you misheard! It's three hundred exactly!"

"Maybe the judge himself doesn't know. That's why he wants her alive—to find out."

"Either way, her children are still orphans!"

"My, my, won't the ravens be happy?"

Poor crow, she must have sensed something was wrong, for she cawed when they took her.

The judge kept his word: He released Butula and Makhara.

While they were leaving, Butula turned back to the judge and whispered in his ear:

"Don't betray me . . . but they brought you another crow."

"What? Another crow?" shouted the judge and ran out. "Either you bring me that crow alive or you'll be fined for deceiving me."

What was left for them to do? They left the judge in distress. To this day they are looking for that crow. They wish that crows did not live three hundred years; that way at least they would be able to argue that the crow had become old and died.

And so they search.

But what does Butula care now . . . He's already dead.

Translated from the Georgian
by Ia Eluashvili

SEAL OF FATE
(FICTION FROM AZERBAIJAN)

SARA NAZIROVA

Sara Nazirova was born in 1944 in a settlement in the Oguz region of Azerbaijan. She received her undergraduate degree from the Pedagogical Institute and her graduate degree from the Institute of Philosophy, both in Baku. Thereafter, she worked at the Art Museum of Azerbaijan for twenty-two years. She was a member of the Artists Union of the Soviet Union until it disbanded and is currently a member of the Artists Union of Azerbaijan.

Ms. Nazirova is a writer, an art critic, and an editor. She published her first short story in 1964. She is the author of four books, one on art theory and art criticism and three works of fiction. Her art reviews, short stories, and narratives have appeared in several Azeri and Russian publications. Ms. Nazirova is currently editorial director of the prose department for the journal *Azerbaijan*. She simultaneously directs the cultural department of *Iurd*, the political, economic, and cultural publication of the presidency of Azerbaijan.

Ms. Nazirova lives in Baku. The following selection is excerpted from her book *Tale damgasi* (Seal of Fate).

Recently, I felt my aunt's spirit so close to me that I couldn't stand it, and I gathered my things to go for a visit. I borrowed a hundred *manat** from a neighbor and set off first thing in the morning. When I reached the village, it was still well before sunset. I decided not to go directly to my aunt's and got off the bus along the post road to walk the rest of the way. The stony road that I had wished to travel alone for my whole life stretched before me like a dry river bed. When it rains, it practically turns into a river. But now, the freshly fallen snow on either side was melting. Big trees along the road seemed as if they had crossed their bare arms, guarding the way like walls of an ancient castle. As in my childhood, I felt the timidity brought on by the quietness, and I smiled. So what was going to happen? I slowed down, caught my breath. Alongside the cemetery, I climbed the embankment and craned my neck to see the darkened tombstones. Perhaps I would be able to see the place where my aunt was buried. Then I remembered that they had not yet taken the covering from her grave. Uncle Shemhal had come to the city and announced, without a word of greeting, "I buried your aunt next to my mother." He had made the statement in a serious and portentous manner as if he had shown my aunt great respect. As if being next to his mother, my aunt would be subdued . . .

My grandmother used to say to me: "Tanri** erected formidable mountains on this earth; from north to south, at every junction. Neither can one person find a common language with another, nor can one nation with another,

---

*manat—currency of Azerbaijan Republic.
**Tanri—the god of the pre-Islamic religion of the Turks. Azerbaijanis are a Turkic people.

nor one government with another. The word of one is unintelligible to another. When it is summer on one side of the earth, it is winter on the other. One face of the globe is night; the other, day. The pristine natural beauty of this world ought to be preserved so that when humans are exhausted from their daily struggles, they can be refreshed by gazing upon this paradise. Yet everything we see is put in a terrible state by the rapacity of humankind. There may come a time when there will not be a breath of fresh air to be inhaled or a mouthful of food fit to eat. Earth, which was destroyed three times by humanity's greed, has reached such a state that Tanri has seen that those who have destroyed their own hearts are now doing the same to plant and animal life. Tanri sent flame and fire and the earth burned. What is the use? Even after millions and millions of years, nothing has changed. The Creator is warning about what he wrought. He is turning the earth upside down. Mountains are turned into lowlands, and lowlands become mountains as a lesson to the coming generations. Are they not the descendants of Adam? The sinner has no redemption. They have turned the surface of the earth into a nest of shame. Tears flow instead of water. Tanri said that you yourselves will know. Run around, if you like, or beg. You have free will, you find your own path. If you do not find it, you drown in your own sedition.

One or two found refuge in Noah's ark; the rest were drowned. For how many years was the earth washed with their tears and cleansed! Now they say whatever calamity comes, it will come from the skies. For our sins, the Creator will take away our air. He will remove it from the face of the earth so that its cleanliness will not be defiled . . . He fills the lands with animals and plants, giving specific flora and fauna to each continent. He created Australia. There lives an animal that carries its young in a pouch on its belly. When you see that creature, you laugh heartily. Even grown-up men are amused. He bestowed something on the four corners of the earth: to deserts, their camels; to India, its monkeys; to Chinese lands, their dragons. Elsewhere are the polar bears and man-eating trees of Africa. To the four corners of our home, he awarded the soil of Turan. Ours is the land of roses, tulips. Inside, a beautiful girl bedazzles the eye, as if it were your image. I hope you will be such a girl when you grow up. Will you be smiling at the world, or will you cry at it? It is not possible to predict. Will you be yearning after the desires of your heart? Who knows what the Creator has in mind? Once in a while the devil urges me to question Him, to demand an explanation for the children with tears in their eyes . . ."

So saying, my grandmother would make the transition from admonition to pity. She would squarely place herself before my aunt, her daughter-in-law: "I do not know what your sins are in this world that you do not receive your share of goodness . . ." My aunt would be hurt, and go out. My grandmother would talk to herself for a bit and then send me to look for my aunt. She would caution me to be careful with my words.

I would first seek the grazing calf. Whenever I needed to be by myself, I would go in that direction. The calf would greet me by lowing as if to complain, as if my aunt's crying at its neck was making it lose its appetite. This time my aunt wiped away her tears. Perhaps to conceal her own sorrow, she asked if I knew why calves always looked mournful. I answered:

"How should I know? They are waiting for their mothers; they want milk probably."

My aunt shook her head. "Oh, no," she said, "they do not know their parents."

"Aunt, where are their parents? Why are they not living together?"

My aunt replied: "Humans slaughter their parents, child; or they use them as beasts of burden, to draw carts. When they are finished with the animals, humans go after each other. They can't get enough of hanging and stabbing, exiling people to Siberia, running into tragedies—so children are left alone."

My uncle arrived when we were eating dinner. My aunt, sitting crossed-legged on the floor, made a move as if to rise. She somehow could not stand up easily and sat down again. Then she rose with difficulty. Using both hands, she tottered like a loaded camel, and pushed herself up. My grandmother at her side said, "Let's get going!"

That night, while sitting with my hand under my chin, my elbow resting on my aunt, I was suddenly shaken to consciousness. Someone pushed my elbow away from my aunt's stomach. I pulled away with astonishment. My aunt's stomach rose on one side and deflated on the other. "Aunt's stomach is boiling!" I laughed. It was as if the hush that had descended upon the house with the arrival of my uncle had been sprinkled with hot water, making the air sizzle. Everyone shifted in their places. Grandmother put in a word: "It is time to pick the watermelons, eh, Shemhal?"

"It is still early, ey Mother," said my uncle, with animation.

In my aunt's presence, Uncle's words "ey Mother" hung in the air like a bridge. Grandmother did not let another silence descend: "A week early, a week late. Come, pick as many as you want and take them, the rest will stay here. Autumn is approaching, all hands will be busy."

Uncle rose as if in a hurry, and said, "Let me go somewhere to sort things out," leaving before my aunt could object . . .

Walking between my uncle and aunt, I realized that if I were not there, they would not have been able to contemplate the peace of the road. Then I understood that what the adults cannot achieve, they blame on children. I had reached school age. If my parents, who lived in a different village, had not come to collect me, I do not know how much longer I could have served as a bridge between my aunt and uncle. In honor of my first day in school, my aunt styled my hair; it was a sight to behold. She carried so much water from the river that she was bent from the weight of it, and she washed my hair one strand at a time. She worked so hard that every time I hear of a coronation I recall my aunt's efforts in styling my hair.

Among all the tombstones bearing inscriptions in the old alphabet*, how could I know which was my aunt's mother-in-law? How could I discover my aunt's resting place next to her? I considered myself educated, yet I could not read their names. The inscriptions were as closed to my understanding as the other world. My inability to read the carvings revealed to me the full tragedy of my aunt's absence. My heart shivered as if ice water had been poured all over me . . . I returned to the road and rebuked myself. What did you expect, fool? You've been hurrying as if to see your aunt. Your heart was high as if, when you walked through the gate, your aunt would come and embrace you. Your aunt is gone. The high road you are taking is leading you, for the first time since her death, to your aunt's house. Didn't it occur to you what that means? Fear of the sadness that awaited me made my knees buckle. Trying to go on, I suddenly saw that I had come to the stump of an old chestnut tree. I sat down on the edge of the stump, only to hear my aunt's voice: "Are you an orphan that you sit alone by the road?" When children sat on this stump, my aunt used to tease them by saying: "An orphan sits by the road and looks at the hands of the passersby."

Despite the force of this childhood memory, I could not move. Even if someone noticed me, I thought, they would not know who I am. It has been so many years since I left the area. I lived in this village until I reached school age;

---

*old alphabet—Arabic.

then I used to visit only during vacations. The people would hardly remember me after so many years.

A strange sensation enveloped me while I sat on the stump. It seemed that this was not the tree-stump I had longed to sit on throughout my life. It was as if I had been born and died on this stump. I had never left it, and all the other places I have been did not exist. All the other days of my life were dark winter days, and these seconds that I counted were an endless ocean.

Many a person had traveled, just as I had. We were all brought to this world to be counted on this land. Ay, ancestors, forgive your children who have lost their way!

I saw a group of people coming in my direction and sprang to my feet. Immediately I regretted my hasty action. Why should I get up for people I don't know? If you wish to sit, then sit. Did someone make you get up? Or is it your aunt or grandmother urging you? Anxiety was in my soul. I forced myself to sit back down. Looking out of the corner of my eye at those approaching, I thought my blood would stop. My aunt and grandmother were among them. As they came closer, I realized I was mistaken. Their clothes, their shapes, and the way they walked had deceived me. It is plain, as they say, that your homeland is your homeland because that is where you see people who look like your mother, your aunt, and all your relatives. Even if they die, others who look like them remain. When the group came close, I looked away. One of the women in the group called out, "Why are you sitting there like an orphan?"

"I got tired, my bag was heavy."

Just then a man stepped forward and asked, "Aren't you my milk sister?"

It *was* my milk brother, the son of my aunt's in-laws with whom we used to play hide and seek along this road. When his mother had died, my aunt breast-fed him. Thus, he used to call her "Milk Mother," even though he had grown up to the size of a calf. The other children began calling her "Milk Mother" too. He now had a mustache and beard . . .

As we entered the courtyard of my aunt's home, he announced me to the household, "I brought my milk mother's niece," as if nobody would have known me by my name. I felt as if he were distancing me from my aunt every time he called me "Milk Mother's niece." In reality, we are both hers. We are her children, who keep the fire of the home hearth burning.

Strangely, although the thought of entering my aunt's courtyard had worried me throughout my journey, it did not matter now. It was as if my aunt had never left this abode. As always, she was presiding over the kitchen fire, and the rest of us were catching each other up on the day's events. I realized that I had been frittering away my time to avoid facing the reality that I was not to see her again. I had expected to confront my aunt's death as soon as I entered the village. The pain of losing a loved one, which I had so far not felt, I would confront precisely there. But the village was as it had always been. With the quiet lushness of its forests and the purity of its colors, it was a paradise cleansing the soul. I had thought that I would fully experience the loss of my aunt in her courtyard. When I did not, I understood that death travels ahead of the individual. In essence, after death there is no sense of death . . . What a person means to you during life, so the person remains. Everything in this house remained as if my aunt were still alive . . . There was the cradle that my aunt carried all the way to the regional hospital, despite the knee-deep snow. I thought of asking for the cradle, to take back with me to the city, to make it the centerpiece of my home, to remember my aunt. Then I realized that there was a robust baby sleeping in it. If he were to fall to the ground, the earth would split open. He was radiant as the full moon. He was asleep, the son of my aunt's in-law's child. Let my aunt's cradle remain full.

The little girl gently rocking her brother's cradle finally overcame her shyness, and asked me, "Aunt, why did you not bring your children?"

I bit my lip. I said, "I do not have children."

"Why don't you?" the little girl puzzled. Not believing me, she insisted, "Where are your children; we could have played together."

"I never had children."

"Why not?"

"I did not have any."

"You did not have them in your belly?"

I laughed. The little girl's mother took pity on me, and said, "You are speaking words taller than your body." She then apologized to me, "The children of today, sister, ask until they get an answer."

"That is all right. At their age we knew and used to play bride and groom," I responded.

Her mother tried to tell her little girl that Aunt was still single: "She is living with a clear and calm ear; she does what she pleases. Is it not sung in the popular tune, 'When I was a girl, I was a princess; when I became engaged, I became a ruler; and when I married, I became a lowly soldier.' Now, my child, your aunt is a single princess; she is not laboring under responsibilities."

But the child did not yield: "I know, she does not have a father, therefore she has no children. Why does she not have a father? Is she an orphan?"

The child freed her hands from her mother. A bit later she reappeared with a zoology textbook and timidly placed it before me. Opening the book, she said, "Aunt, look, this has a child; why do you not have one?" She was pointing to the photograph of a monkey embracing its offspring. I almost fell over laughing . . .

Translated from the Azeri
by Audrey Altstadt

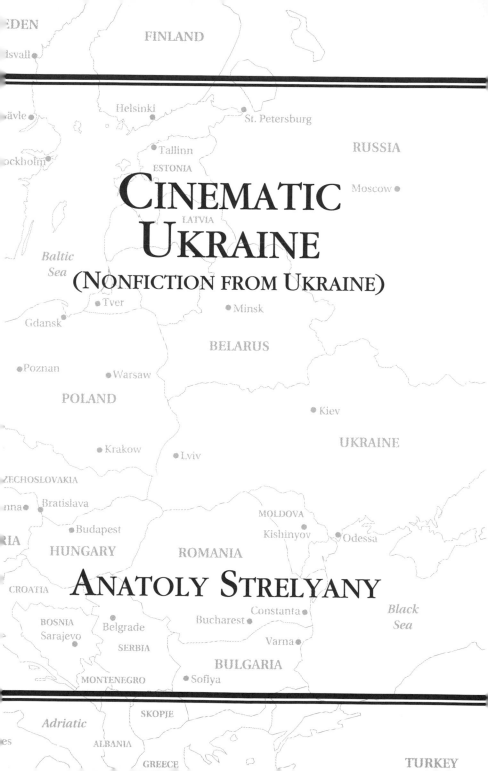

Anatoly Strelyany was born in Kharkov, Ukraine, in 1939. In 1971, he was graduated from the Journalism Department of Moscow State University. He subsequently worked as a tractor operator in Kazakhstan and as a journalist in Moscow and Siberia. He was an editor at the publishing house Soviet Writer, and for a year was the head of the science section at the newspaper *Novy Mir*.

Mr. Strelyany is a prize-winning screenwriter. Six of his films have been produced, two comedies and four documentaries. In 1989 he was awarded the State Prize for Cinematography for his documentary *The Peasant of Arkhangelsk*.

Mr. Strelyany is an essayist and the author of twelve books, both fiction and nonfiction. He has published essays and short stories in a variety of literary journals, including *Oktyabr'*, *Literaturnaya Gazeta*, and *Iunost'*. His writing has been translated into Bulgarian, English, French, German, and Polish. The following selection is excerpted from an essay that originally appeared in the literary journal *Druzhba narodov* (Friendship of Peoples).

Mr. Strelyany lives in Moscow.

*O*n *March 17, 1991, a referendum was held throughout the Soviet Union, although only nine of the fifteen republics officially participated. The essential question was: Do you consider it necessary to preserve the USSR as a renewed federation of equal sovereign republics in which the rights and freedoms of people of all nationalities will be fully guaranteed? In Ukraine, citizens were also asked to vote on a second referendum: Should Ukraine abide by its declaration of self-sovereignty of July 1990?*

Some time ago, my Austrian colleagues and I spent a month traveling in Ukraine, filming a documentary. This was our third trip: The first two times we went in the summer and then realized that we had no snow on film. Since winter is a significant part of the Ukrainian scene, we felt we should have it on the screen.

On March 9 we went to my native village, between the towns of Kharkov and Poltava, to film the celebration of the last day of winter. It was 20°F, snow covered everything, and the winter sun was just peeking over the horizon. In the main square, near the *klub*, or community center, they had erected a freshly planed wooden pole. Anyone able to climb it all the way to the top would receive a prize. The smooth yellow surface of the pole seemed to radiate cold air. We shuddered as we watched the brave souls who struggled almost all the way up only to slide back down, their naked stomachs rubbing against the frozen wood.

We sent a camera aloft on a hot air balloon to shoot the winter landscape. The kids enjoyed it, and it provided plenty of gossip for the adults. Most of them took us for aliens. But what amazed us was that the moment the balloon went up, it was noticed immediately. To tell the truth,

I did not expect so many of my fellow countrymen to look up at the sky . . .

Making a movie is an exciting but nervy business no matter where you do it, but particularly in the Ukrainian countryside. You have to film ten people to show one, and interview one for an hour to get just a few seconds of footage. You wait for sunny weather and search for the right angle for days. Then, when everything seems ready, it inevitably starts to rain, or a herd of cows barges in mooing, or a man comes up and asks whether you are from Poland and might have something for sale. That is one kind of trouble. The other is when somebody starts asking whether you have a permit to film there at all.

In Drogobych, we were filming in the courtyard of the Pedagogical Institute, where they had recently begun excavations of secret burial grounds. Just before the beginning of World War II and for a long time after that, the Institute was headquarters for the Ukrainian branch of the NKVD*. The "enemies of the people" from the surrounding area had been brought there. Those who were executed were buried right there in the yard, or thrown into the well.

Among the recovered skeletons with bullet holes in their skulls were the remains of school children eight to ten years old.

Here an old man kept pestering us. He had on a worn-out blue gown, the type usually worn by the people who are responsible for the keys in government buildings. "Who let you in here to film?" he kept asking anxiously. "Didn't you see the sign on the gate saying that passersby should stop and remember those who were tortured here?"

"We *are* passersby," I said, "so we stopped."

"No, you are not *just* passersby." He was staring at us stubbornly and with anger, but his fear was gone. He

---

NKVD—predecessor of the KGB.

would report this to his superiors, he threatened. I asked him why he, an old man, should trouble himself, climb upstairs, and bother the authorities. Did he have to? "Who knows who put up the sign," he said with hatred.

In one village in the Khmelnitskaya province we spotted a bust of The Leader. It was a very impressive head, big and yellow. It was resting on a pedestal in a park, not in some backyard as we had seen many times in other places. While we filmed in the park, there were only kids around us, watching. As soon as we trained our camera on the head, however, a woman appeared, out of breath and wearing a shawl thrown hastily around her shoulders. "Who are you?" she asked. "Do you have permission to film here?"

"And who are you?"

"That does not matter!"

This was typical. Never would they introduce themselves before questioning us. Likewise, suggesting proper introductions usually infuriated them.

"Still, who are you?"

"I am the store supervisor here. That is my office over there; I saw you from the window."

Sometimes it seemed these people had supernatural intuition.

On the Soviet-Hungarian border we had picked up a demobilized Russian officer and given him a ride to Mukachev, in West Ukraine. He was in a sad predicament: His Russian Volga, which he had bought in Hungary and was driving home, broke down just before he reached the border. He was covered with mud, unshaven, and exhausted, but not upset. Born in Barnaul, Siberia, he had been graduated from a polytechnic school in Lvov, in West Ukraine. As we drove, we discussed national issues. He told us that non-Russian soldiers are insulted when referred to as the "Russian Army," as many would like to call it again. They went to serve in the *Soviet* Army, they insist. The officers don't care so much. Most of them are Russian anyway, and the rest are aware of the historical tradition to accept foreigners in the Russian Army.

"The main ethnicities we have are Russians, Ukrainians, and Belarusans." The officer was educating my Austrian friends, assuming that they knew nothing about the Soviet Union. "We are like three branches of the same tree. Not all the Ukrainians agree with that, though, and most of those who don't agree live here, in West Ukraine. They consider themselves a separate nation. So they call me *moskal** or *katzap*, and I call them *hohly*, but it is clear that no matter how much they try to separate themselves, we are all the same nation, all from the same cradle. We have our diligence in common. Or rather, our lack of it."

Speaking of which, he praised the Balts, also without dividing them into nationalities. "They are more advanced than we are. They are like Germans. Calm, Nordic people. Decent and industrious, but very vindictive. The way they got back at us after the war! They slaughtered whole families, so we sent them to Siberia. I lived there for a while, side by side with them. They work so hard! But they are very reserved, closed people. They don't even think about drinking, just about their work and families."

Every nation that wishes to leave the Soviet Union should be allowed to secede, he says. But the separation should be genuine. For example, what was given to the Lithuanians should be returned to Belarus. Let everybody secede, no big deal.

"We let Finland go, didn't we? We released Poland, right? Those very Balts, we let them go first, then took them back, devil knows why. Even Georgia was let go, then taken back. We should let them all go, for good."

He gave his foreign audience time to appreciate his gen-

*moskal and *katzap*—offensive terms for a Russian; *hohly*—offensive term for a Ukrainian.

erosity, then added: "And then, when they start asking to return, we should consider very carefully whom to take back. Very carefully! So that they realize that they have made a mistake. And then—take them back, of course."

In his opinion, everybody would be asking to come back. Everybody except the Balts.

"The Balts will be all right by themselves. They have a sense of responsibility. The rest, they need somebody to be in charge of them and take care of them. I know; I worked and served with them. The Georgians, of course, are very developed people. Armenians too, nobody argues with that. Armenians are very good with their hands—they can forge anything, including gold. But they are not very responsible. The Russians are themselves a lazy bunch of hacks, especially in basic training; but if you give them a good whipping, they will do anything. All the rest—it doesn't matter whether you whip them or not, they just don't care."

The Austrians were having a great time listening to him. Our people usually did not speak so openly in front of foreigners. Just before we arrived at Mukachev, they asked him whether he realized that he was talking like a chauvinist, despite his good humor. He disagreed, but immediately changed the subject to the Americans:

"They've got it right. There is no such ethnicity as American, but there is an American people. They have come from all over the world and just get along. If we had states instead of republics, we would have no trouble either."

"So how are you going to vote in the Referendum?" I asked before he got out.

"For the Union, of course. I am supposed to."

The war invalids spoke out most colorfully, especially in East Ukraine.

"Ukraine, Russia—same crap," one veteran was talking, pounding on his wooden leg. "Let them live as they wish: together, apart, by turns. As long as people have life: have stuff to eat, to drink, to smoke. Take Brezhnev's time. Everybody ate, drank, and had a good time. He himself had fun too, traveled like a king, went to India and everywhere, ate and drank till he belched!"

Despite his talk, he would not tell my foreign friends how he was going to vote.

"I am afraid. Who knows who you are?"

"If you are afraid, why not simply say that you are for the Union? Otherwise, it shows that you really are 'against'," I said.

"Does it really? No, I am 'for', honestly."

Many people still fear Soviet power like a plague. I believe there are many more frightened people than any sociological study would reveal. Judging from what we heard on the road, everyone was sure that even from an "X" scribbled in place of a signature on a ballot, *they* could find him and make his life miserable somehow—take away his pension, for example.

On March 17, Referendum Day, we were in Odessa. We stopped at several voting stations. The one we chose to film at was in a blue-collar district, near a large factory. People went to the polls with enthusiasm: There were groceries for sale at the station.

"What did you buy?" I asked a woman leaving.

"Everything! I bought some smoked cheese, sweet cheese, buttermilk. I got some soda water too!"

The woman was middle-aged, red-cheeked and happy.

"If it is not a secret, may we ask how you voted?"

"I voted very good! For the Union, for our Ukraine, for the Referendum," she counted, gesturing. "Everybody should stay together; then everything will be good. It will be very good. Two years will pass—you will see how good everything will be!"

"What was written on the ballot?"

"I don't remember, really. I read it, but I already forgot.

Maybe I'll remember later, but if I don't, I am still sure that everything will be fine. Our Union is very strong!"

Translated from the Russian
by Sonia Melnikova

Soviet citizens voted in support of the all-Union referendum, but not overwhelmingly so. Ukrainians voted to uphold their declaration of self-sovereignty. Five months later, on August 24, 1991—five days after the coup attempt against Gorbachev— Ukraine officially declared independence.

THE SHADOW OF A FLYING EAGLE

(FICTION FROM KYRGYZSTAN)

KADYR OMURKULOV

Kadyr Omurkulov was born in 1941. In 1965, he was graduated from the Screenwriting School of the All-Union State Institute of Cinematography in Moscow.

Mr. Omurkulov worked in Kyrgyzstan as chief film editor for the State Cinema Studios (GosKino) and later as chief editor at KyrgyzFilm Studio. He worked at the State Committee for Television and Radio Broadcasting (GosTeleRadio) on the script board and later as director of KyrgyzTelefilm Studios. He was Kyrgyz bureau chief for the Soviet press agency Novosti for seventeen years. Mr. Omurkulov was president of GosTeleRadio's successor, the State National Television and Radio Broadcasting Company of Kyrgyzstan, until recently.

More than thirty of Mr. Omurkulov's screenplays have been made into feature-length and documentary films that have received wide acclaim at home and abroad.

Mr. Omurkulov is the author of a number of books that have been translated into several languages. He was honored for consistent journalistic excellence by the publication *Druzhba narodov* (Friendship of Peoples). He is an Honored Artist of the Kyrgyz Republic.

Mr. Omurkulov lives in Bishkek.

Sheraly decided to ride his horse home and not to wait for the truck from the hippodrome. He made up his mind about it even before the games began, right after he arrived in town and discovered what was bothering Chaar. The horse's hind legs, above the fetlocks, were covered with blood. Knowing Chaar's temperament and that of the two other horses in the back of the paneled truck, he should have foreseen that.

Perhaps the driver of the truck drove too fast and rough and scared the horses, or they just did not get along and hurt each other; who knows? Nobody saw what actually happened. When Sheraly found his horse in the stable, resting after the trip, Chaar was hanging his head and walking around in circles, as if reproaching his master and complaining about his pain. Sheraly treated Chaar's wounds and blamed himself: To hell with that truck. Never mind that it is more than two hundred miles, he was going to ride back home on horseback. He realized that it would mean three nights on the road, and only on the fourth day would he reach his *ail*, or village. He had plenty of friends and relatives living along the way. It would be no burden for them to put him up for a night.

Sheraly ground some burdock leaves and spread the sticky green stuff over the horse's wounds. Everything seemed to be going well: Chaar was calming down, and the eagle had been doing just fine during the trial flights, reaching the running hare very fast. Still, Sheraly was not in a good mood. All that fuss before the contest, the shouts of the game organizers: "Release the hare! . . . Go, go! . . . Left! . . . Right! . . . Release the eagles! . . . Next hare! . . . Now eagles! . . ."

There was no particular reason to get upset. It was always like that before the games. Still he felt sullen; even the noisy pot-luck supper with fellow *sayachi*, or falconers, did not help to shake off the nagging feeling.

During the games, when the large crowds gathered, he became incensed. The audience was shouting, applauding, cheering on the *sayachi*, who stood in a tight group atop a high wooden platform. The impending eagle hunt caused a storm of joyful excitement in the stands, which echoed and rolled all the way down to the field. Sheraly found himself beside the cages of animals meant as bait for the birds. His attention was especially caught by the desperate look in the eyes of a young fox with a small sharp snout. The organizers were trying to prod it out of the cage with wooden sticks. The fox was resisting, trembling with fear and bracing itself against the metal bars. At last they forced it out and then someone kicked it in the ribs so hard that the fox was sent flying to the field. The audience whistled and jeered, trying to get it to run for its life to escape the eagle. The *sayachi* was swinging his arms, teasing and warming up his bird. The small yellow fox was shaking like a falling autumn leaf, turning its head endlessly as if looking for somebody. Too confused to run, it was crawling sideways. When the fox caught sight of the eagle, it spread on the ground and froze, seeming to have breathed its last even before the eagle could reach it.

Next they let out a wolf. With a heavy head and a hard predatory look in its eyes, obtuse snout covered with a muzzle, the wolf was still young but already showed its good pedigree and promised to become a powerful animal. It walked out of the cage and started on an easy run along the green field, seeming comfortably in its element, as if all this commotion had nothing to do with it: all these people crowding in the field, the *sayachi* on horseback and the cheering stands. The wolf looked at ease, moving masterfully on large paws, stretching, and enjoying the fresh country air. But a few minutes later it became clear that its calm was only apparent, that it was not missing anything.

The *sayachi* threw his bird high up, and toward the wolf. The eagle took the start with a few powerful strokes and then folded its wings, stretched its neck and flew like an arrow. It had almost reached the animal when, at the very last moment, the wolf sprang aside and the eagle fell heavily, wings sprawling on the grass. The wolf, knowing that the eagle could not take off without a man's help, paid no more attention to the bird that a minute ago was its mortal enemy. The eagle flapped its wings helplessly as its unsuccessful master rode toward it. The crowd laughed.

A second eagle was already circling above the wolf. Next instant it froze in mid-flight and fell like a stone thrown into an abyss. One could actually hear the air hissing. This time the attack was precise. However, the wolf overcame the pain, and was now trying to bite into the bird's throat, only to discover that the muzzle prevented it. Whining in frustration, the wolf hit the bird with its heavy paw. The eagle shrieked, but wouldn't let go. The wolf rose up on its hind legs and fell with all its weight on its back, crushing the bird underneath. The eagle's wing must have been twisted, for it released the wolf. The wounded animal was not in a hurry to escape, however. It shook its head, trying to get rid of the hateful muzzle.

Now it was Sheraly's turn. The game organizers called his name and signaled him with their hands, but he would not take the hood off his bird. This was no longer a hunt, but the torture of an animal. He could see that the other *sayachi* were frustrated with the wolf and were pursuing him on horseback. The wounded wolf could not express its rage: Its jaws were tightly locked by the muzzle so it could not even show its fangs. It could only howl and bite its own tongue. The *sayachi* drove the wolf into the bushes and started lashing it with their whips. Gathering its remaining strength, the bleeding animal sprang up onto one of the riders. The horse shied and shook off the rider. Another *sayachi* struck the wolf on the head, the blow sounding as if it had hit metal. The wolf whirled like a top. The fallen rider jumped up and finished off the animal . . .

Sheraly, who had not unhooded his bird after all, stepped down from the platform. He felt very tired. No, he decided, he was not going to make the long trip here and take part in the games any more. Let the youth show off their skill and daring, Sheraly thought as he left the field; he was finished. Excited horsemen rode next to him, discussing the games. Sheraly was quiet and sullen, so they left him alone.

Next morning Sheraly was already on the road. Another *sayachi*, Mokesh, was traveling with him. It would take them a day to reach Mokesh's *ail*, where Sheraly would stay overnight. They had known each other for many years but saw each other only during the games. Mokesh was good-natured and easy to get along with, but when he drank he became loud and tiresome: He couldn't say a word without tugging your sleeve or nudging you. Sheraly did not mind having him as traveling companion, however; a long way gets short when you are not traveling alone.

At dawn they walked their horses out of the stables, got onto the main road, and left the sleeping town. The early morning chill made them shiver in their saddles until the sun rose.

They stopped at a roadside restaurant. While Mokesh fetched some beer, Sheraly bought some raw meat. He took the hood off his bird and started feeding it. With its strong hooked beak the eagle tore off pieces of the meat Sheraly held up for it, his hand in a leather mitten. The bird's bulging red eyes reflected the sun rays.

Mokesh brought two mugs of beer and two half-glasses of vodka. He was annoyed with the idle gawks who started gathering around and shouted at them:

"Go away, this isn't a circus."

The crowd moved back a little and watched the birds from a distance.

"Let's have a drink," Mokesh said, raising his glass, even though he was well aware of Sheraly's solemn vow never to drink alcohol when handling his bird.

That happened more than twenty years earlier. Sheraly had been hunting with two of his birds, one of which was Azoo.

When Sheraly was still a barefoot boy, his father found the nestling among the rocks on the tip of Azoo-Tash—Raging Cliffs, named for their frequent rock slides. They named the bird Azoo, after his native mountain. He was now very old, Azoo, but still in his full strength, God bless him. He must have eaten something bad, though, just before the games; he had to stay home this time. Doubtless he was sitting on the old stump at home, waiting for his master . . .

It was Azoo who had sliced his master's cheek with his claw, sharp as a cleaver. Sheraly suddenly had had a hunch that something treacherous was coming and he looked up into the sky to see the bird circling. He managed to escape the direct impact of the eagle, who was aiming right at him.

Sheraly wondered later what exactly had caused that fury. Perhaps he had shown off too much in front of the other *sayachi*, nudging and clapping his bird on the chest harder than usual. But most likely he provoked it when he forgot that the eagle couldn't stand the smell of alcohol and kissed it on the beak. Whatever the reason, Sheraly had sensed that something was wrong even as he threw the bird up; it was slower than usual and seemed reluctant to take off.

But Sheraly was not fast enough to escape. He managed to throw the bird off, but only after it had cut his cheek open. Azoo fell, his mighty wings sprawled helplessly on the ground. Sheraly's startled horse reared, and the wounded Sheraly lost his balance and tumbled onto the ice-covered ground, right next to his bird. He sprang to his knees, ready to fight, but the eagle was motionless. It watched its master wipe his bleeding cheek with snow. The bulging eyes did not blink. The two stared at each other for a long time, until the *sayachi* knew that it had been his fault. He felt like a father guilty of hurting his innocent child. It was time to offer peace. Sheraly picked up a handful of snow and started eating it. The snow did not really satisfy his thirst, but little by little it cooled his boiling blood. Maybe the bird was thirsty too, he thought. Slowly, the *sayachi* approached the bird and stretched out his palm full of snow. And the bird accepted it. At that moment Sheraly pledged never to drink any time he was with a bird. He never broke his vow.

It did not matter to Sheraly that not everybody understood. "This is not the worst thing in life," he used to say, smiling with embarrassment when they made fun of him.

"You are our hermit saint." Mokesh grinned, baring his chipped teeth through the thin red beard. "We all are sinners compared to you, and we should pray on the hem of your clothes to cleanse ourselves . . ."

"That's enough now, let's go. Everybody is watching," Sheraly said and stood up.

"I mean, your hem, get it? Ha-ha-ha!" Mokesh laughed at his own joke, tugging Sheraly's sleeve and thumping him on the stomach. "On the hem!"

"You will not be comfortable on my hem." Sheraly tried to pull his friend to his feet.

"Why? You are a saint, and it's a tradition, isn't it?"

"Be a man, Mokesh-bey, you know why, let's go," Sheraly could not hide his irritation.

Mokesh was trying to steady himself and at the same time to pick up his hooded eagle from the back of a chair with his gloved hand, but he kept missing. The bird was helplessly flapping its wings and stretching out its neck.

At last, the drunken master lost patience. He let out an angry curse, grabbed the bird in his arms as if it were a chicken at the market, and walked out of the restaurant behind his friend—still somehow managing to hit him on the side with a spare hand. All along he mumbled drunkenly:

"Hey, do you want to buy this bird from me? Someone offered me a ram for it. No? As you wish, you will regret it later. I already got two sheep for two of my hawks. This one I am saving for myself, it provides for me. Recently it caught a fox for me. Its fur was red as fire. I traded it for a ram . . ."

"You must have a whole herd by now . . ."

"Herd or no herd, but my pen is not empty. Who needs this hen-coop otherwise!" Mokesh said, clapping his eagle on the wings. The bird looked forlorn and tired and drew in its neck in fear.

It took Sheraly a long time to help his friend up onto his horse. Then Mokesh stopped talking and dozed off.

Sheraly spent the night at Mokesh's and left at dawn. By noon he had already passed the narrow Bom ravine, and he decided to give his horse a rest. He turned toward a small cozy house next to the railroad crossing, in a clearing between the tracks and the river. He drank some tea from tin mugs with his friend, a pointsman, shared some news, and said good-bye.

By evening Sheraly was approaching Lake Issyk-Kul. The tireless gusty winds were blowing at the port town. The wind was so strong that Sheraly could feel his horse wavering under him. The wind calmed as soon as he moved further inland. Sheraly picked up his pace, trying to get to Toruaigyr before nightfall. He was going to stay overnight there, at the lighthouse. His old friend Turdumat, the lighthouse keeper, put up his *yurta** right at the shore from spring through fall, so as not to travel back

---

*yurta—igloo type traditonal tent covered with felt.

and forth between the lighthouse and the village. Even though he was very old, Turdumat refused to give up his job. He had been keeping the light on for almost forty years, from the time when there was only a kerosene lamp burning on the top of the tower.

Sheraly approached Turdumat's *yurta* at dusk. A fire was burning in the hearth outside and meat boiling in a copper. The keeper's grandson greeted the rider, led away his horse, and invited him in. At the same time a boat touched the shore. Sheraly could see Turdumat and a young man in a white cap in it. Sheraly helped them out.

"You never know what trick life will play on you next," Turdumat joked after greeting his friend. "Look at this fellow: He wants to write for a newspaper about me. It has been torture for both of us!"

"We are done for today," the young man said apologetically. "Get some rest now, it was hard indeed . . ."

"I am just kidding, son. I should not be the one to complain. It's you who are wasting your time here for two days because of some silly old man. You must really need me for something! There must be dozens of other old bearded men with poked faces like mine on the shores of Issyk-Kul . . ."

The young man was obviously interested in Sheraly and his eagle but was trying not to appear too eager. He knew that the guest was staying for the night and there would be time to talk.

"You are a good traveler, Sheraly," Turdumat said when they had made themselves comfortable inside. "You must have been traveling with good thoughts, since you arrived just in time for supper. Now, tell us what's happening in the *ail* . . ."

The conversation was floating peacefully, warm as the light of the oil lamps. Even though the young man was not from around there, he knew more about this land than Sheraly himself: that not far from here, on the bottom of the lake, were buried the walls of an ancient city; that Issyk-Kul, according to the scientists, used to be much larger, and that the Chu river, which no longer reached the lake, used to enter it. There still were traces of dry river bottom there. Sheraly learned many other things from him that night. The visitor said that his name was Taasir, that he was studying in Moscow to become a journalist and was interested in the old legends that had "true roots."

"How can a legend be true?" Sheraly inquired politely. "Legends are like fairy-tales, aren't they?"

"No, a legend is not a fairy-tale. It's often proven that old tales really took place. This is the kind of story I am looking for here: the tale about Toruaigyr, the Bay Stallion."

"*Barakelde*, my son," Sheraly was deeply moved. "I confess that I thought the young people didn't care about old tales and legends any more, that they had other interests now. I thought all they cared about were cars. As for Toruaigyr, the Bay Stallion—maybe he did exist, and maybe not. . ."

"Still, what do you think?"

"I think he did; otherwise how come they named this shore after him?" said Sheraly.

"Exactly. And if it was true—what a miracle it was when the Bay Stallion escaped his herd, which had been driven away by the enemies, and swam all the way back across the lake! If it were in my power, I would build a granite monument to him here."

"The way you are telling it, it was a miracle indeed . . . Life is more interesting if you believe in miracles. I remember well the day when my father told me that once while I was asleep in my crib, I was touched by the shadow of an eagle flying high in the sky. Whether it was true or just one of my father's legends—who knows, but I took it in, and that is how I developed my passion for eagles and the hunt. I liked so much to think that the shadow of a soaring bird had indeed touched me that eventually I believed it. This faith is what made me a *sayachi*."

That is how Sheraly started his story that night. He sensed that he was not wasting his words, but planting seeds in fertile soil. Taasir listened intently.

Every fall, Sheraly explained, the *sayachi* set up their nets to catch eagles, kites, and hawks. It is the season when the birds are passing through on their long journey from the banks of the Issyk-Kul to the countries of Arabia and Indochina. The *sayachi* place a live wild pigeon as bait into a little hole in the ground, cover the hole with a net, and camouflage the net with leaves and branches. A raptor circles in the sky and then rushes down like an arrow on its victim—that is the moment to pull up the net fast. Nothing compares with this languishing waiting; you feel as if you are hypnotizing the bird.

The real *sayachi* tames the bird even before he catches it, while it is still in free flight. Taming may sound easy but it is long and tiring. A *sayachi's* patience and devotion to the birds is tested. Many exhausting days and nights pass before the bird submits to the man's will. In the beginning the bird will not accept food from its master's hands. It will not even eat in his presence, preferring to starve than give in. But, continued Sheraly, the hunter knows that the worst thing for an eagle is lack of sleep. He tries to keep the bird awake, but it can be very clever, sleeping with one eye closed and one eye open. A hawk is easier to tame: As soon as it is thirsty, it becomes as obedient as a sparrow. However, trained hawks are more treacherous and lazy. When they are not hungry, they only pretend to hunt. The eagle is most difficult to train. Once tamed, however, it is most devoted to its master. There is an ancient belief that when a *sayachi* dies, his soul moves into his bird, which sometimes lives to be a hundred years old. After the master's death, the bird stays in the master's house to remind the family of the deceased, and everybody takes care of it.

It is not easy to be a *sayachi*, Sheraly said. Often you wander for days in the wilderness, among the rocks, looking in the cliffs for an eagle's nest, and then have to fight for a nestling. Months, even years will pass before the bird learns the hunt. And all this time the bird needs fresh meat. It is not uncommon for a *sayachi* to neglect his own family while taking care of his bird. Some people say that a real *sayachi* should do nothing else, for he just does not have the time for anything else.

"Because of these birds I had to give up teaching geography in school," Sheraly smiled sadly. "I work as a maintenance man now, so as not to lose my pension. Smart people used to laugh at me openly, but I didn't pay any attention to that, so they stopped, even though they still tease me sometimes . . ."

"I disagree with you, Sheraly," Turdumat interrupted, "I think people envy you a little bit. Everybody respects you and turns to you for advice. No herdsmen leave for the winter pastures without your blessing. Your advice is like a talisman for them: They know that a *sayachi* is close to nature and knows everything about it; even the wild eagles obey you." Turdumat remained silent for a while, as if listening to the lake waves sighing outside in the midnight darkness, then continued:

"Sheraly hypnotizes an eagle at first sight. Newly caught birds take food only from his hands. Some people even think that he knows some magic. That is just silly talk, of course. He has it in his hands. The way he touches a bird, it must think it's a touch of its mother's wings. He also knows how to touch the bird so as to feel that special thin layer of fat, which means the bird is still too young for the hunt. That fat should melt away altogether before the bird can become a fast hunter . . . Not everybody has such a gift as Sheraly. God grant him many years."

Old Turdumat was talking about him, but Sheraly did not seem to hear him. He was watching the dying flames, but must have been far away, deep in his thoughts about the birds in the sky . . .

They talked like that late into the night. Sheraly eventually fell asleep, but before the stars faded he was already up. He left the *yurta* quietly, trying not to bother the sleeping.

He did not wake up the young man to say good-bye: They had agreed to meet later on top of Azoo-Tash, where he had his nets set up. He was surprised that he felt so close to this young man and was so open with him.

Sheraly untied his horse and, refreshed with the chilling wind from the lake, started down the road.

It was just before dawn when Sheraly reached home. The streets were empty and the village was still asleep, but ready to awaken at any minute. For some reason, though, the lights were on in his windows, and that alarmed him.

His wife, his Salima, was a very quiet woman. Nobody in the village ever saw her arguing. But she was not shy. Salima had been a young and fragile girl when she followed her heart and against her parents' will entered Sheraly's house as his bride. Since then, no matter which way their life turned, and no matter what Sheraly did for the sake of his passion for his birds, he never heard a word of reproach from his wife. Salima never pried, never tried to talk him out of his passion, never asked him to give it up and live "like everybody else." She was proud of what they had: their family and the children, who respected her and her husband and did not ask for more.

His wife met Sheraly in tears and could not even begin to tell him what had happened. He sensed that something very bad had occurred, but he did not rush her. Wiping her face with a corner of her head-scarf, she brought some *airan*, or yoghurt, mixed it with cold water, and handed the bowl to Sheraly, to welcome him after the long journey. Now he was ready to listen . . .

The night before last, their son had brought home a bride, a daughter of the veterinarian, Alymbai. She had come of her own will, and Salima had covered her hair with a white bridal scarf and blessed the young couple. They decided to wait for Sheraly to come home, so that they could go together to the future in-laws with the good news. But yesterday at dawn Alymbai himself showed up, together with some of his relatives, and tore the scarf from the young bride's head. She pleaded with him not to, but he was in a rage and would not listen. Instead he shamed her and shouted: "What a father in-law you chose! Who does not know Sheraly: He lives among rocks like a wild goat, he sleeps in the caves like some vagrant! Even at such an important time as this he is devil knows where, he cannot even come to request marriage for his son! You will spend your life here feeding his birds! I don't need an in-law like that!"

And Alymbai had taken his daughter away.

"Did she go with him?" Sheraly asked, looking down at his hands.

"Yes."

"Well, so be it. She is not a right match for our son."

"I think Alymbai got upset because our family did not come to him to ask for his daughter in marriage . . ."

"So be it . . . Why are you still crying?"

Salima sobbed again and became quiet.

"Go ahead, tell me what's the matter. I'm listening."

"Go outside, you will see . . ."

Outside in the yard, the truck was where his son had abandoned it last night. The front wheels had torn into the fine fence behind which Sheraly's oldest bird, Azoo, usually perched on an old stump.

There were wheel tracks on the dewy ground. And there lay the crushed eagle, its wings twisted, covered with dried blood and mud.

Sheraly, clenching his teeth and fists, hit the car hood

with all his force. A kind of soundless moan burst out of his throat, neither a cry nor a groan. He felt as if leaden weights lay heavily on his shoulders. As if in a bad dream, Sheraly approached the stump and lowered himself to the ground. He sat, grieving silently, scarcely hearing his wife's words.

"He was drunk," Salima was saying, trying somehow to soften it. "He was not himself from the shame and humiliation; he did not realize what he was doing . . ."

Sheraly spoke at last. "I feel so foul in my soul . . . can't see him . . . don't let anything bad happen . . ." he said, as if casting a spell.

He picked up a canvas bag and gently, as if trying not to cause pain, wrapped it around the dead bird. Then he walked to his horse and, with difficulty, mounted.

"I am going to Azoo-Tash. Tell my son I shall be waiting for him there."

Slowly Sheraly rode out of the yard and crossed the small street of the village. He was out of breath, overwhelmed with rage and grief. But hope flickered within him that there, on top of Azoo-Tash, something magical would happen. Suddenly, he urged on his horse, exhausted after the long journey, and sent him galloping toward the mountains.

Translated from the Russian
by Sonia Melnikova

DON'T BE FOOLED!
(NONFICTION FROM ARMENIA)

ARAMAYIS SAHAKYAN

Aramayis Sahakyan was born in 1936. Mr. Sahakyan began his literary career in 1958 with the publication of his first volume of poetry *Astghikner* (Little Stars). He published several volumes of poetry. He later turned to journalism and in 1984 published a satirical collection of "Amusing Interviews." Mr. Sahakyan is senior editor of the popular satirical review *Vozni* (Hedgehog). He is the author of four books in Russian as well as a number of translations from Russian into Armenian. He has received several awards from the Armenian Writers Union as well as an All-Union diploma.

Mr. Sahakyan has been a member of the Armenian Parliament since 1989.

Mr. Sahakyan lives with his family in Erevan.

T his sharp critique of the former Soviet regime in Armenia, rife with cynicism, reveals something of the trauma the Armenian Republic experienced in the aftermath of a devastating earthquake on December 7, 1988. Many of the refugees still lack adequate housing. Their numbers have been swollen by hundreds of thousands of ethnic Armenians forced to flee the Azerbaijani capital Baku in 1990. Since then a virtually complete Azeri economic blockade—occasioned by the conflict over who will control Nagorno Karabagh, the Armenian enclave inside Azerbaijan—has resulted in a serious decline in Armenian living standards. Consequently, though the current government in Armenia was elected with a strong popular mandate in October 1991, this has been steadily eroded. Thus the piece still reflects the underlying mood of disillusionment in Armenia. Having outgrown its initial euphoria over independence, the electorate once again faces extremely harsh conditions, this time under the rule of a parliament it finds curiously unresponsive to its basic concerns.

When will there finally be justice?

Over the past few days I've been speaking at length with people in the Nork' Massif and in Jrvezh, suburbs of Erevan, trying to help them at least in some small way. Every night I return home with a question tearing at my heart: Why are they so unfair, so heartless toward one another? I suppose the cruel circumstances make people coldhearted. I even remind myself that every neighborhood of the Nork' Massif lacks a thousand necessities. For example, an ordinary telephone. What's trivial about that? Those who live on the outskirts of the city need a telephone. But those who can make and receive a call by telephone in the Nork' Massif are few and far between. The way people are treated there is a mess. The name Jrvezh derives from the word 'water' (*jur*), but Jrvezh hasn't got any. There's no public transportation. There's no radio. Armenia's highest officials are to blame, those who look out from their magnificent political heights but fail to see the heights of Nork'. Politicians visit and promise solutions, but it seems it's too windy and dusty a place: The wind whisks the promises away with it . . .

A ludicrous situation results. Individuals who do not benefit the population in any way speak in the people's name. They speak on behalf of Armenians, the very people they harm. They speak in the name of the nation, but cause the names of the nation's youth to be lost. Some have closed their minds and opened their mouths. And the naive among us are fooled.

There's an epidemic of talk, an earthquake of discussion. When politicians talk too much, nobody listens. In the past we would at least have shown the speaker some respect. No longer.

But they continue to talk. They even talk at industrial plants for the deaf and mute! Everyone wants to tell others what to do. But what's the use? What's the use when our boundless country gets 17¢ a hectare compared to England's 67¢? What's the use, when there are two hotels per thousand people in our country compared to twenty abroad? What's the use, when 34 percent of our population works in agriculture and the country's principal problem is nutrition? Socialist cows give ten times less milk than capitalist cows because our treatment of them is inhuman, that is, the way we treat humans. Ideological organizations are made responsible for solving economic questions. Our leaders have continually promised mountains and not even delivered molehills. They've fooled us, claiming we're very rich, and we've believed them. We've fooled them, calling ourselves fortunate, and we've believed it.

After regarding ourselves as a rich, fortunate state for

years on end, we now discover that in a worldwide standard of living survey we occupy . . . forty-sixth place. We boast about our love for our little ones, but there isn't one children's hospital in all of Armenia.

Don't misunderstand me. I'm not of the opinion that there's nothing powerful in our country. Far from it. Why, look at our bureaucracy. Who else has such a powerful, developed bureaucracy? Each year the government consumes a hundred billion sheets of bureaucratic forms. In our country we do not have a cult of personality, but of forms. And who says we're not first at something? We're first in the number of speeches made out of what could be said in one breath. Our country ranks first in the world for its number of inspectors. Inspectors outnumber those inspected! And who says there's nothing permanent in our life? Far from it. Why, permanent lines, permanent 'temporary' difficulties. Who says there's no expansion or progress here? Aren't bribery and injustice expanding at an enormous rate? Who says markets are few? Aren't bureaucratic institutions the real market where jobs, apartments, money, etc., are sold on a grand scale? Some regard such institutions as their personal haciendas and treat everyone else as slaves. We understand their exploiting a building or a factory; but to exploit the nation's patience?

Let's recall that no one is anyone's slave. We're all slaves. However, many have no interest in working, because that does not increase their income. That's why some people expend all their energy on *not* working. Abroad, it's the person who works who has a life; here it's those who don't.

Someone recently purchased a defective product in which there was a handwritten note: "Workmanship reflects payscale." I don't think it's right to judge that worker, but the system that created him. To blame the foreman for the shoddy buildings that collapsed in the earthquake is not enough; you ought to blame the poor system of economic planning and construction. We decry the poisoned air, but it is not the air that is at fault, but the factory that produces the toxins and the people who back it. Most of our mistakes are a result of the system.

But when one leaves aside the big issues, we are collaring each other, pointing fingers at one another.

We have an epidemic on our hands. At meetings people are exposing one another, bringing to light stains on their records, all in the name of "promoting *perestroika.*" Well, do your exposé, but it is necessary to ask as we take each step: Does this benefit the nation? Throughout our age-old history, our leaders have often tried to fool us, and we have often been fooled. Whatever they have said, we have believed. Then we tossed the "Armenian Question" into the world's jaws, and it chewed and consumed us. It's always afterward that we realize we've been fooled. Now, too, we're being fooled. Our leaders are deceiving us in masses . . . and laughing to themselves. Hasn't our blind love of all our leadership been foolhardy? Our leaders have always dragged us backward.

But everything has an end.

People have been fooled so often they've lost faith in justice. I understand how a person can fool someone for seven hours, seven days, but for seventy years? Deception is a crime, of course, but allowing yourself to be deceived is no less a crime.

I know one political candidate who addressed the voters as follows: "Good people, if you elect me deputy, the next minute I'll reunite Karabagh, I'll fill up the stores [with products] and Lake Sevan [with water], I'll improve the environment, reduce the waiting lines, abolish earthquakes . . ." Women were particularly moved when another candidate swore, "After being elected deputy, I'll devote all my powers to ensuring that every woman has more than ten children." Sweet words. But people grow bitter from them, for there is no sugar on the shelves. The unhealthy aspects of our life are not the result of a shortage of soap, but an excess of people on soapboxes. Soap supplies have declined, but the number of soft-soapers has not . . .

Stalin wanted to create a rich country with a poor population; the poorer they were, the greater their dependence. And so socialism became the society of the poor. Whoever strove to live well was labeled a *kulak** and was squashed under Stalin's *kulak* fist. Living well was regarded as something bad, even "anti-Soviet." The poor were considered fortunate. Hence the Soviet people were the most "fortunate" on earth. A poor, callous country was created. Anyone with a bathtub in his house was sent into exile for being "bourgeois." The stores were empty; the inscription over the doors read, "Glory to the Party." After Stalin's demise, poverty remained. Many decisions have been made, but decisions don't keep the wolf from the door. In agrigulture, we sow and reap more bureaucratic forms than crops. Ration stamps for butter, meat, and coffee stamp out our belief. Space is full of spacecraft, but the stores are empty—the opposite would have been better. It is like holding a wedding and having no bread to put on the table. The hammer and sickle are emblazoned on our ensign and flag because the hammer and sickle is the level at which we've remained.

The problem of apartments is next after the problem of food. Even the houses have no hot and cold water. In Jrvezh one person said, "My grandson looks at the bathtub plumbing and asks, "What's that?" Perhaps if we pour hot water over the director of the water utility that doesn't deliver hot water, there'll be hot water.

Our leaders direct the least attention to the most important things: health care, education, culture. They create an object for trade with the speed of a gazelle, for culture at a tortoise's pace.

But justice is our greatest deficit. That too comes from

---

*kulak—a peasant who owns land and works for his own (instead of the state's) profit.

the Stalin years. (At this point, some would say, "Enough of continually taking Stalin to task." I agree. If you are courageous, criticize the unjust leaders of today.)

Stalin should be condemned, so that his kind does not return. I think Stalin made no errors; only an innocent man can err. He is a villain of global proportions: How can one call what he did "errors"? Hitler, a fascist, did not wipe out as many Communists as the Communist Stalin did! I'm surprised Hitler wanted to wipe us out, when Stalin was already doing a good job of it. Even the greatest genius is not pardoned for murder.

But we still like the fist. We deceive ourselves. The callousness evident in certain people today is a result of the unspeakable callousness of three decades of the Stalin regime. And why would one not be callous? The Communists destroyed churches, ruined monasteries, considered the Bible harmful, accused people's friends of being "enemies of the people." Law enforcement agencies broke not only people's spirits, but their bodies too. Where did all that callousness originate? Scientists have discovered that many murderers tormented animals in their childhood. For them, affection was deemed weakness, goodness a defect.

It is not enough that space is polluted; it is not enough that our planet is weighed down with armaments; it is not enough that people are dying of heart attacks, cancer, AIDS, drug abuse, internal and external diseases, poisoned air, water, and soil, robberies and murders: We also wipe out one another with envy, spite, and careerism.

When there is war in the world, humanity is mindless. Seeing tanks during peacetime hardens people's hearts. People are getting worse. Still, goodness will save us.

An old woman pensioner whose seven sons had given their lives in the war protested that a well-heeled young man had demanded a hundred rubles before he would give her the fifty-ruble pension she lived on. We talk big

about the earthquake casualties and victims of the mas-
sacres at Sumgait and Masis, but we have left them totally
helpless. I saw a youth who had lost a leg. "They're asking
a bribe for crutches," he said. How can one bear it, when
they demand a bribe from earthquake casualties, when
they demand it of orphaned children? They steal the
clothes sent for the naked, the provisions sent for the
starving, the homes for the homeless, the patient's medicine. What can we do so that people will again believe in
justice? There is one way out: to act justly. Two million
crimes here remain hidden, unprosecuted. Some of the
infractions were committed by guardians of the law. If
those who uphold the law are lawless, people are lost . . .

For years on end we've treated monsters like angels.
How did it happen that cruel and unjust men like Lavrenti
Beria, N. I. Yezhov, Sharaf Rashidov, Kunan, and Geidar
Aliev became the country's leaders, members of the
Politburo, recipients of the Order of Lenin, Heroes of
Labor? How did it happen?

Revolution begins when people no longer believe the
authorities.

We live in a time when seeing a decent person, we don't
believe our eyes. How can a decent person exist here? If
he's not on the take, how will he pay off those above him?

When I spoke out against injustice on television, a terrible witchhunt started up; when I mentioned that I was
reconsidering my attitude toward activists in the
Dashnaktsut'yun party and certain West Armenian writers
viewed with suspicion by the Party, a new political cen-
sure began; when I questioned Comrade Rishkov of the
Politburo about the status of the Armenian people, some
became afraid—because bureaucrats are as afraid of sharp
minds as sick persons are of a corridor draught. They're
the same people who named the naval clinic after Lenin's
wife, they hounded from the Party anyone who entered a
church, they're the ones who demanded politics from love

songs. The eleventh century poet K'uchack wrote in praise of a young woman's body; contemporary writers, of the Party's governing bodies.

Bureaucrats claim to be in favor of political demonstrations, but in fact they oppose them (sometimes demonstrations oppose politicians, too). Bureaucrats are afraid of even the smallest gatherings: poetry evenings, football games. Previously their minds were taken up with organizing jolly meetings: Now they're out of their minds with fear. They repeat others' senseless words saying that the Armenian people are wily. They are afraid to say that the condition of an Armenian in neighboring Turkey over the last several years was better than in our neighboring fraternal republic, Azerbaijan. We are fooling ourselves. Don't be fooled by our leaders' pretty but perfidious words.

If we hadn't been fooled, we'd now be fifty million, not three million.

Don't be fooled.

Translated from the Armenian
by S. Peter Cowe

ECLIPSE
(FICTION FROM KAZAKHSTAN)

RAMAZAN TOKTAROV

Ramazan Toktarov was born in Pavlodar, Kazakhstan, in 1935. He received an undergraduate degree in French language and literature from the former Institute of Foreign Languages in Almaty.

Mr. Toktarov is the author of nine novels and numberless stories and articles. He is a senior editor at the journal *Zhuldiz* (Star), where he has worked for five years. The following selection is excerpted from his most recent novel, *Akboz atty eles* (Bright Recollections).

Mr. Toktarov is married and has three children. He lives in Almaty.

In the book from which the following excerpt is drawn, the author relates the severities of Stalinism in the 1950s. His work speaks with a voice whose credibility stems not, as in the past, from ideology but from a new literary freedom.

Rauan, the pride of the Kazakh-Russian School, completed the ninth grade with honors. As he entered tenth grade, he changed his name—and resigned himself to the consequences.

Rauan rejected the surname of his adoptive parents, Kapezov, for one that had once appeared on a long list of "enemies of the people," Esbatyrov. It was the name of his father, who had disappeared one night many years before.

It would have been safer for him to lie low and change his name after finishing school, but it was not in Rauan's character to do so. As the saying goes, "Feed the wolf what you will, he'll still return to the forest."

"You ungrateful trouble-maker!" yelled Kaskyrkoz Kapezov, who had raised Rauan from infancy. "I'll throw you out of the house! I'll make you a beggar!" he raged.

"Dear citizens," the official radio announced, "tomorrow there will be a solar eclipse. Do not be afraid. Although the sheep may bleat, it is a natural phenomenon. At the time of the eclipse you can use lanterns."

"What is this 'eclipse'? Where does the sun go?" As the time for the event approached, some shut their doors and windows and hid themselves in their houses.

Rauan knew about eclipses, although astronomy had been introduced at the school only recently. As Mr. Kabysh, the teacher, drew the moon's orbit on the blackboard, Rauan grew impatient. He already knew that an eclipse was the passage of the moon between the earth and the sun, the extinguishing of light.

"Mr. Kabysh is drawing Asima's hat," Rauan whispered loudly. He said this to impress Kamila, whose attention he now had, and because Mr. Kabysh had been keeping company with Asima recently.

"What is so funny?" Mr. Kabysh demanded of the class. "Why are you laughing?'

No one dared to say, of course. But after class Irashken, who never kept his mouth shut, told Mr. Kabysh the whole story.

Mr. Kabysh was young. Although he had not managed to graduate from this very school, he had been a good pupil and was now a good teacher and a kind man. But learning of Rauan's remark, he bridled with anger.

He pulled Rauan aside. "What did you hope to gain by this comment?" he asked resentfully. "When I was a student we'd never have dared such disrespect."

"Only . . . to make the girls laugh," answered Rauan without wavering.

"Whom? Silly girls? Or Irashken?"

"Sir," Rauan protested, "I swear, it was a mistake. I ask your forgiveness."

Mr. Kabysh grew nervous. "You meant me harm," he said. "I won't forget this."

"Harm?" asked Rauan.

"You will report to the parents' meeting," he said angrily. But then he thought better of it. Rumors spread like wildfire, and besides, the laughter of the previous hour was nothing compared to what one could expect if it were brought up at a school meeting. Mr. Kabysh dropped the matter without further comment.

Rauan was genuinely sorry. Yet he could not keep silent when he saw others' foibles.

The eclipse occurred the next day as predicted. At first, only one edge of the sun darkened. Later, the children ran outside to gaze at the heavens. Stars glittered in the darkness, startling cattle and dogs. Uneasy bellows and howling resounded throughout the valley.

Only the narrowest rim of sun could be seen. The light of this corona seemed brighter than the sun itself, as if all its light were concentrated into this narrow outline. After a few minutes the shadow crawled from the face of the sun. The spell that had overtaken both man and beast was broken. It was not night, but day. It was time to work.

Adults shook their heads worriedly. The sun is more vital than food. How could an eclipse not bear some evil portent?

Years ago, also around the time of the spring thaw, there had been an eclipse. As everyone stood bewitched, a man named Aksakal had shouted, "Peace in our day, and to our King!" Afterward someone had asked: "Aksakal, old man, what king are you referring to? Have you forgotten that we live under Soviet rule?" "One who lives like a god, isn't he a king?" Aksakal had responded. "If you want peace, wish him long life." Those words, spoken years before, were now remembered.

As everyone's eyes readjusted to daylight, shouting could be heard from the houses.

"Joseph V. Stalin, the leader of the world proletariat," the radio announced, "is near death." He had lost consciousness. It was February 4.

"What will happen if he dies?"

"We are lost!"

"Pray that he doesn't die. Could he have been the king of such a nation had he not been as clever as forty men?"

"We are surrounded by enemies!"

"The American imperialists will swallow us . . ."

All thoughts were of Stalin, who hovered near death.

Rauan shared these thoughts. "If Stalin dies, who will sit in the Kremlin? Who will lead? Where on earth is there another like Stalin, whose lead so many countries have followed without hesitation?" In his diary Rauan wrote:

February 4, Wednesday. Today is a most difficult day for the Soviet people. Our great leader, Joseph Vissarionovich Stalin, is dying. He has suffered a brain hemorrhage. He is paralyzed on one side, his heartbeat is irregular. The radio says that all of his bodily functions are impeded. His condition is critical.

February 5, Thursday. Our leader's condition is changing for the worse. Doctors hope that his heart can hold out. His temperature is 101.5 ℉. He is still in a coma.

What will happen to us if Stalin dies?

February 6, Friday. Today Kamila wasn't in class. She has never missed before. Nobody seemed to know where she was, but I didn't ask my classmates; I was afraid they would tease me. Anyway, one shouldn't think of such things on a day of national tragedy.

When we were in physics class we heard a cry in the corridor. My heart skipped a beat. We all rushed outside, following Mr. Abdirash.

"Our great leader," someone announced, "the great leader of all progressive humanity, Joseph Vissarionovich Stalin, is dead. He died yesterday at 9:50 pm."

"Farewell," I said, as if in a dream. "Farewell, Comrade Stalin."

As the news was announced a man turned to Mr. Abdirash and looked into his eyes:

"Didn't you hear? Stalin is dead! There is no leader . . . no leader!" The man rushed from the schoolyard.

Rauan almost fainted.

Back in the classroom, stunned boys and girls bent their heads over their desks. Some wept bitterly. Others cried loudly but without feeling. Rauan was still. His eyes were dry.

Irashken, who always sat in front, suddenly began shaking with laughter—not from nervousness but from genuine amusement. "Why are you all crying? Are you nuts?"

Mr. Abdirash was livid. "What are you saying, scoundrel? Do you think we are pretending?" he demanded.

But what is said is said; the spell was broken. Some students at the back of the class began snickering. "Why are we crying?"

When the bell rang, the students went to join the mourners in the streets. Here people stood like fish on an ice floe; they wept and wept, as if the universe were coming to an end. Even the factories mourned, their shrill whistles mingling with one another.

Among the scribblings in Rauan's diary that day was something he had once heard: "A man casts two shadows, one on the ground, the other on humanity. The second is his destiny." For Rauan, ten years of studies would end today. Was it possible that *all* life should stand still? "Does the Irtysh River still run its quiet course?" he wondered. "I must see for myself. I must go and see." Rauan gave his school bag to a younger boy who lived in the neighborhood. He followed the multitude in the street without knowing where.

Suddenly, Rauan found himself in the central park, where mourners had gathered. Some expressed their feelings at the rostrum. A woman next to Rauan in a fox-collar coat cried aloud and fainted. Rauan looked into her pale face but couldn't rouse her. Someone doused her with water. Recovering, she asked:

"Oh, where is he? Is it true?"

Walking through the park Rauan saw others who had fainted. Suddenly he noticed a girl walking calmly. She wore a dark-blue coat. Was it Kamila?

Yes!

"Destiny," he thought. Of late he had forced himself not to glance at Kamila in the classroom. Whenever he met her, he nodded in greeting, but nothing more. Kamila was not aware—or didn't want to show that she knew—of Rauan's feelings for her.

Lord forgive him, but on this momentous day Rauan had thought of little *but* Kamila. How many minutes, hours, and days had he dreamed of her, this proud young woman? The year before he had composed a poem for her but had never dared to give it to her. Now she walked toward him. She laid her head on his shoulder, eyes welling with tears.

"Rauan, forgive me," she said. "I was born into sorrow."

"What happened? Do you mean Stalin?" asked Rauan.

"My father, my father!"

"Everyone's father," Rauan corrected her. "You are not the only one who suffers . . ."

"No," she interrupted, taking his arm. "My father was arrested yesterday." She began to sob.

Rauan grew silent. He knew that Kamila's father was the director of a *kolkhoz.** Such an arrest left little cause for hope.

Kamila pulled Rauan from the crowd. "My mother is at the *kolkhoz*. We need your help . . . "

"Your mother . . . How did you find me?" asked Rauan in a daze.

Kamila smiled. Her eyes, still wet with tears, were gorgeous.

"I followed you," she said.

"You were looking for me?" he asked.

"My mother sent me to bring a classmate to her. She will tell you everything herself."

On the day that Stalin's long shadow passed from the land, Rauan felt that he, not Kamila's father, had been arrested. Henceforth his own small shadow would paint the land and point his destiny.

Translated from the Kazakh
by Usen Suleimenov

---

kolkhoz—Soviet collective farm

MALVA'S STORY
(FICTION FROM LITHUANIA)

ZITA ČEPAITĖ

Zita Čepaitė was born to a farming family in Taurage, Lithuania. In 1984, she received an undergraduate degree in philology from Vilnius University.

Ms. Čepaitė is the author of two books. The first, published in 1987, is a collection of short stories, *Atsvaitas* (Reflection). Her novella, *Sekma Skausma* (Pain), was published in 1989.

Ms. Čepaitė has traveled extensively. She regularly participates in international conferences focusing on women's rights and is deeply involved in the women's movement in Lithuania.

Ms. Čepaitė lives in Vilnius. She is currently at work on a novel.

All ill-fated love stories consist of three parts—initial attraction, infatuation, and disappointment—and are all similar and equally dull. If someone decides to confide such a story, you feel trapped: Although you might guess all the details in advance and hear stereotypical, even identical phrases, you mustn't betray even the slightest irritation. In an especially unpleasant variation, the storyteller (women in particular are likely to seek compassion) begins to weep and complain that her life is over, her soul has been trampled, the world is horrible and deceitful. Seeing the creature quivering like a bowl of jelly, you realize that you ought to console her, that the Lord himself commands that you console her, but you also realize something else—that your consolation will lack sincerity.

We're not accustomed to analyzing what we call "private life." And yet, the discovery that what we imagine to be a unique experience has been gone through by many would help some of us overcome the oppressive burden of feeling misunderstood. It is only when you consider yourself and your own situation as unique that you see others—who have presumably never experienced anything remotely similar and could never even conceive of your suffering—as enemies. We are more alike than we imagine, and that likeness is not as shameful a thing as our originality-worshiping age claims. This hatred for the crowd is the result precisely of individualism that is rendered too meaningful—imagining that the difference between the shape of my thumbnail and my neighbor's is more important than the citizenry's demonstrations for bread or freedom. The world is packed with worthless things—people have managed to transform many things into trifles—and it's strange how a quivering creature turned into jelly encourages one to contemplate the hopelessness of the human situation. If this creature is a woman abandoned by her lover, her descriptions of a destroyed life, however trivial, are not groundless.

A woman abandoned by her lover . . . Sounds like a novel. But I'll try not to become too involved. As befits a woman of my age, I will speak candidly, hiding nothing, but justifying nothing either.

Her name is Malvina. Malva, for short—that's what everyone called her. Her mother chose the name. I never heard the girl complain, but I could see that she suffered because of it. Sure, the kids teased her: "Malva Schmalva, Malva eats halva." I once explained to her that any name could be made fun of, and any word could be made funny. Twelve then, Malva listened to me with wide eyes. I'm not sure why I'm paying so much attention to her name. In these days when silly things have become the fashion, and flippancy has become the norm, the mellifluousness of a name should no longer matter. Take a look at fashion: short and wide culottes, jackets flared at the back with sleeves barely covering the elbow, a brightly colored knot tied carelessly at the neck, or a wide, loose, fluttering scarf—a scarecrow's costume if I ever saw one! Now add hair that's cut to ear-length—silly-Willy hairstyle. I can't imagine a justification for such pretentiousness.

"The dumber the better," snapped a teenager once when her mother and I were discussing these things. Without telling her mother, the daughter had pierced an ear and begun to wear one earring. Her mother was an educator who knew that punishing her daughter would accomplish nothing. She brought the girl to my apartment, pretending that they were just stopping by—although we had planned it in advance—and sat her down to listen to our conversation, which, among other things, turned to the topic of morality. We called some things inappropriate, stupid, and frivolous. Others, proper, good, and meaningful. The girl was supposed to listen to our conclusions and decide how to behave and conduct her life. That was the lesson plan. She, however, stared out the window, fingering her earring. Her expression seemed to say that she had already lived through ten lifetimes and knew full well that her teenage escapades were much more real than our pontifical sermons. She seemed drawn to that uncontrollable impulse for freedom and power that others might see as insolence, shamelessness, or recklessness.

Although it's not appropriate to speak ill of the deceased, Malva's mother too had reckless tendencies. Pregnant, she'd walk around with an expression that seemed to say that she could control her swollen stomach, making it protrude even more or completely contract. I visited her just out of the hospital (back then I had no problems getting around and no premonition of my present helplessness), and she behaved as if she had given birth not because the baby had been conceived and eventually had to be born, but because her decision to give birth would make a point or negate something. Being childless myself, I find it difficult to say what a new mother's attitude ought to be, but I did know that she shouldn't gloat over her heroic deed. When I asked her what name she'd chosen, she shrugged her shoulders, looked at her husband and at her daughter's little shriveled-up face, and blurted out laughing, "Why not Malva?" I saw that she was enamored with the power of creating a living being and granting it a name. Perhaps she was mocking the whole idea of it.

Malva was orphaned at age four. She'd drop games with her friends, run over to my apartment, sit where she was told, and fix her eyes on me as if waiting for what I had to say. I understood that some day I would have to tell the girl that her mother had committed suicide, but I kept putting it off. I kept waiting for the right moment—when she was grown-up, mature—until finally, one day, I understood that she already knew everything. Eventually her visits became less and less frequent. On one occasion, when I asked her not to bad-mouth her stepmother, she left, slamming the door behind her. She grew up. She married. She had a daughter of her own. I saw her quite big with child another time, but later I didn't see another little one in tow—I supposed that some misfortune had befallen her. Later I learned the baby had been stillborn.

As for me, I was debilitated by one illness after another. Hospital stays and sanitariums followed. Now I barely inch along. With two canes for support, I hobble to the grocery store.

During one such exhausting excursion I ran into Malva after many years. She was promenading with a miniature Lithuanian tricolor flag clasped in her fist. She was returning from a public demonstration, and her gleaming eyes revealed the same insolent challenge of her mother's face when she was pregnant. We got to talking. She was surprised by my crutches. She walked me to my door, but said that she couldn't come in. She had to hurry home— her husband would scold her for returning late while he and their daughter awaited her hungry.

"After every one of these rallies," Malva told me later, "I feel like I'm soaring. After being part of the crowd I feel as though I've accomplished everything in my life that I can dream of accomplishing. A man in the street once tried to tear the flag out of my hands. I raised it above my head and started laughing. The little shrimp kept spitting and jumping up and down around me. His spit hit me in the face. I was worried that some of it might have landed in my mouth—I mean, I'd been laughing with my mouth wide open. To this day I seem to remember swallowing something."

She was giddy with joy and full of contentment and hope. She was overwhelmed by a feeling dangerous for a thirty-year-old—she was in love, and the rallies and the flags were merely symbols that had brought her and her lover together, made them close, and would finally separate them.

Malva started visiting me almost daily. With fire in her eyes, she would tell me about the Soviet occupation of Lithuania in 1940, the subsequent annexation, the deportees sent to Siberia in 1941, the hunger strikes, and the demonstrations broken up by the police.

"That's when I felt an indescribable desire to own a weapon. A machine gun to blast them with rounds. I'd line them up in a row and fire . . . "

Such passionate, furious outbursts really frightened me. Probably because my physical helplessness prevented me from getting to even one demonstration, not to mention that by the time I arrived, I wouldn't have had the strength to yell, "Freedom for Lithuania!" or "Shame, shame!" And of course, if anyone were to have attacked the crowds there's no way I could have escaped without broken bones; either the crowd would have trampled me or crowd control would have beaten me up. Perhaps it's only what you yourself can't handle that seems dangerous (or even abnormal).

When I saw Malva's resolve, I understood that no one could restrain her or convince her otherwise. She neglected her husband and her daughter. At night, she'd stand vigil at the hunger strikers' huts. She'd picket any government office that Sajudis* summoned her to.

The time I ran into Malva with the tricolor flag in her hand, I hadn't fully grasped what was actually happening in Lithuania. My TV set was broken, and I had neglected to have it repaired. Besides, I'd never been much for watching TV. Malva took the initiative, and in just a couple of days the TV was working perfectly. (I was surprised by Malva's zeal. I could still remember when, as a child—

*Sajudis (sy' yu dis)—literally, "movement." Sajudis was a political organization urging the independence of Lithuania. It subsequently became a political party.

even a teenager—she'd sit where I left her, not even changing her pose. And here she was brimming with energy and determination.) Malva persuaded me to watch certain programs. She'd tell me which newspapers to read and when to listen to the radio. I could see that she was yearning to draw me into this whirlwind of events, hopes, desires, disappointments, indignation, and rage.

"Don't you feel that your life is passing you by against your will? Yes, of course you do!" she yelled. "Has anyone missed you during these ten years when you've struggled just to walk? They didn't even care if a wheelchair was made available to you. And even if you had one—where would you go? That's how the system works! They want to shove us all into little cages so we won't be able to see or hear anything."

Yes, I was handicapped, and no one needed me, not even Malva. Incidentally, she didn't realize this, but who cares? When we're young our sorrows and losses shape our world. I had grown accustomed to my cage, as Malva called it, and had a completely different understanding of what that cage was. But I didn't want to argue with her, I didn't want to upset such solid and clear convictions. Her insensitive declarations confused me, but all the same I found them charming.

"You see? You're crying. You understand now that you've been dominated and oppressed. They wanted to destroy you even though you weren't the slightest hindrance to them. You hardly existed. And yet they wanted to destroy you."

But I had begun to cry because I remembered how, after her mother's funeral, her childishly attentive eyes had pierced me, making me feel duty bound to tell her the whole truth. We now embraced and sobbed. Apparently, she wept out of pity for me, thinking that I had finally comprehended my true condition. I wept because—with my exaggerated caution—not I, but strangers, had informed the girl about her mother's suicide. It was as if at this very moment I was feeling the trembling of a little heart, too young to comprehend all the horror of a suicide.

It was during that conversation that Malva admitted she was in love. She spoke of her husband who didn't understand her and who had completely won over their daughter. Whenever Malva wanted to speak with the girl, the father would linger in the doorway and brusquely interject that she was already grown-up and that there was no need to spin fairy tales.

"I'm not spinning tales; I just want to tell her about Lithuania."

I learned that Malva was attracted to a fellow named Roland, and as it happened, quite unaware, I had served as a kind of go-between, helping them to get acquainted. A distant relative of mine from America, who happened to be Malva's age, had come to live with me. Lithuania was not Julia's main interest—just one drop of Lithuanian blood flowed in her veins, and that was well diluted with Russian and Spanish blood. Rather it was social problems, the condition of handicapped children and of women. I was useful to her in many respects. She lived with me and could observe the problems I encountered daily and the privations that made my life difficult. I had introduced her to Malva, and they had quickly become friends.

Julia didn't speak Lithuanian, but her Russian wasn't bad. Her degree was in Sovietology, and she'd taken courses in Russian. She and Malva attended demonstrations together, Malva acting as interpreter. It was Julia who introduced Malva to Roland; she had asked for an interview with him for an American newspaper.

That evening all three of them stopped at my house. The talk centered on politics—the goals of freedom and independence and a return to the rule of law. For the first time in my life I was frightened that a listening device might have been planted in my apartment. I suddenly felt important: In my average, quiet, and wretched two-room apartment something significant and heroic might be occurring, even if it was just an interview for the *Washington Post*. Julia's questions were short and to the point. She sometimes impatiently cut off Roland's poetic and generalized ramblings. Malva sneered at the questions and greedily drank in Roland's responses.

While they talked I made coffee. It was twilight, but I hadn't turned on the kitchen light. Leaning on my crutches, waiting for the kettle to whistle, I felt my own powerlessness more clearly than ever before. Seemingly I had already come to terms with it; I might even add that there were certain advantages to my lameness. I burned my hand as I poured water from the kettle, and I called Malva to come get the coffee. Although the others invited me insistently, I refused to come out of the kitchen myself. I was suddenly ashamed of my handicap, guilty, as if it weren't disease that had defeated me, but I that was responsible for my lameness.

That night I barely noticed what Roland looked like; he was tall and well-proportioned and had a long, narrow face. He was keen on using vivid figures of speech, aware that they impressed his listeners. He spoke in parables: about the giant with clay feet and the mouse in the elephant's ear, about the necessity of bringing love where no love exists and peace where there is conflict and vengefulness. I later told Malva that those words were just poetic metaphors. She didn't believe me. She grew angry and screamed that I didn't understand anything. In her yearning for love and peace, she was ready to believe any promise.

I knew that Malva and Roland were having an affair. Her husband threatened her with divorce, but she paid no attention. She stayed away from home for weeks, at my house or a girlfriend's. She'd beg me to let her have Roland over—and I would. She'd demand that I call and tell him she was ill and wanted him to visit—I'd do so. Without my realizing it, Malva had turned me into a madame. She and Roland would lock themselves in her room where I knew they were making love. She filled my cripple's apartment with the passions of a lively and healthy person.

One day, Malva's husband came looking for his wife. I told him she wasn't there, but he kept looking through the open door. Seeing that he didn't believe me, I invited him in to wait for her. He sat on the sofa and folded his hands on his knees. He was balding—the shape of the back of his head had become apparent only after he'd lost the hair on top. I offered him coffee and tea; he wouldn't utter a word. I realized that he didn't want anything to do with me. After an hour or so, he glanced at his watch and left.

On another occasion, her daughter came. She pierced me with her attentive, unblinking gaze as Malva had done a dozen years ago. Without even asking whether her mother was here, she turned and stormed down the stairs. That week, Malva was apparently sleeping at her friend's house, or perhaps she had gone away with Roland. When she returned, I told her that her family had missed their little homemaker. My ironic tone angered her. She refused to speak to me or eat. She desperately tried to call someone on the phone. Then she went to her room and slammed the door. I knocked, opened the door, and said:

"Even someone who's in love should obey some fundamental rules of civility."

"Rules of civility!" Malva laughed out loud, "What rules? Tell me one!"

"When you enter a room full of people—even if they're complete strangers, even if you're fighting with them—you should say hello. And when you leave the room, you should say good-bye."

Malva was stretched out on the couch, her face to the wall, laughing.

"When someone asks you a question—even if that person is your worst enemy—it's rude to answer with your back turned."

Malva's laugh was becoming hysterical.

"You shouldn't cut people off, no matter how stupid and unworthy of your time they may be."

More laughter.

"Render unto Caesar the things that are Caesar's and unto God the things that are God's."

Though the laughter had become forced, it continued.

"Whosoever of you is without sin should cast the first stone."

Malva quieted down, glared at me, then began twisting her head as if she were choking or resisting a tight collar.

"That rule you just mentioned," she said ironically, yet sincerely, almost ashamed, "is not so fundamental."

I understood that she wanted to make up but couldn't find the words. I sat down beside her and put my hand on her thigh. She began to pat it gently. Later, after she'd had some tea, she called her husband. At first they seemed to speak calmly, but later Malva's voice became louder, her words more capricious. I heard her say that she was free and had the right to choose her own lifestyle and values. I finally understood that not just Malva's husband and daughter but everybody—including Julia and me—were interfering with the free and unhindered lifestyle she wanted.

Julia was a horse of a different color. Julia told stories about Chicago, New York, and Los Angeles. She had spent time in each of these cities. She later lived in Europe for a couple of years, where she studied at several universities. Malva, one could say, had never left Vilnius, not counting one almost obligatory excursion to Moscow and a few summers spent at Pioneer camp in Giruliai.

Another difference was that Julia tended to listen, observe, and analyze—the opposite of Malva, who enjoyed talking, explaining, and proving things. These traits may have been related to the women's respective professions. Julia, the sociologist, saw human beings as objects worthy of careful investigation and detailed analysis. Malva, the educator, saw them as imperfect, faulty beings that must be taught and trained. I admit that Julia's outlook was more to my liking. I prefer diversity, however unattractive, to cookie-cutter perfection. Furthermore, in Malva's eyes, everyone was an enemy threatening her freedom. Julia looked at others as she looked at herself—as free participants in a life overflowing with purpose.

I'm not sure whether Malva noticed these differences. She was convinced that she and Julia were very similar, and she prided herself in thinking that she was Western in outlook and free of the Soviet slave mentality. Julia fully understood the differences. If not for her, the friendship between the two women would not have been possible. In a word, she knew how to adapt. A Soviet-educated absolutist would say that Julia had no face of her own. About fifteen years ago, I'd have said the same thing; now, perhaps because of my illness, or perhaps because I'm aging, I'm more likely to compromise. Thus, I prefer kindness to integrity. I dare say that I've seen more than my share of genuine faces, and the majority of them are hardly worth talking about. Julia's ability to get along fascinated me. After living in Lithuania for only half a year, she had already acquired a good number of friends. She had more than do people born and raised here, including Malva, who barely knew how to make new friends and was rapidly losing old ones.

As a matter of fact, the question of companionship and friendship was extremely difficult for me too. I kept asking myself, "Am I worth the effort? Am I a nuisance?" Especially after my illness, I felt as if nobody needed me. When my former colleagues visited me in the hospital, I told them that I didn't need their charity. And look at me now—I'm jealous of Julia's ability to befriend the occasional passerby who stops to chat. I'm watching her and learning from her, though I realize that never in this life will I get the chance to benefit from the lessons. Julia's research of the Soviet system took her on many trips to Russia, especially Moscow. Every time she returned and recounted her impressions, I expected to hear her gripe about the Soviets and their ways of doing things, but she only laughed at the discomforts she'd experienced during her trip and marveled at the people's helpfulness and generosity. She raved about how incredibly cheap everything was.

"For a dollar I could dine in a first-rate restaurant!"

She behaved like a child who'd found herself in a storyland inhabited by elves. But to me those creatures were anything but fairies and often quite hard to tolerate. She would talk about the romance of the lonely, abandoned Russian Orthodox churches, about the sad beauty of the dilapidated monasteries, the bleak, endless grass- and briar-covered landscapes, and the crumbling, ivy-covered walls of Vilnius' Old Town, an inspiration to many a painter.

"Life is difficult here, Julia."

She patted my arm and promised to buy me the things that would make my condition a bit more bearable—a wheelchair, medicine, and various medical supplies—in America, where she was planning to go for a few months.

"What I'm trying to figure out is how one can eliminate all that makes life difficult without compromising the beauty," she said, as she caressed my hair and wondered how I kept it so thick and soft.

Malva rarely showed any affection. To tell the truth, I realize only now how I yearned for a caring gesture. I had always considered it, if not indecent, then at least peculiar, for a woman to touch another woman. I was unnerved by Julia's rushing over to kiss me on her return from Moscow.

I wondered if she might be a lesbian. I consoled myself that my age and lameness disqualified me as an appealing partner. I was, however, quite nervous for Malva and was consequently overjoyed by her crush on Roland. I even encouraged more frequent rendezvous, telling them not to be bashful on my account. Malva didn't understand my behavior, and I didn't explain. Now I can clearly say that back then I preferred that Malva be the lover of a patriotically minded Lithuanian man than of an American woman with obscure ethnicity, questionable views, and indecent desires. I was unwittingly encouraging one situation by doing everything possible to avoid another. But my calculated behavior did more harm to me than to anyone else because it was based upon unfounded suspicions and mistaken assumptions—Julia was not a lesbian. (As Julia herself later told me, she didn't return to America to take care of urgent matters, but to make up with her boyfriend, with whom she'd fought before leaving.) After Julia was gone, I breathed more easily and began to press Malva about their friendship. What Malva described to me seemed to have a double meaning: whispers, gentle words, a tendency to compliment Malva's body.

"Did she try to fondle you?"

Malva shrugged. "One time in the sauna she touched my breasts. She told me they sagged a bit and showed me some exercises for firming them."

Then I tried to find out if Malva knew what a lesbian was. Malva made a sour face. I couldn't tell whether she was frowning or laughing to herself.

"Don't think I'm talking about Julia. It's just that—you know—things are changing. You'll encounter lots of new situations."

"It looks like I'm already encountering them," Malva grinned.

"What do you mean?"

Malva raised her eyebrow, explaining nothing. The next

day she went back to her husband. A while later, however, she was back again, asking for a place to stay. Sometimes her daughter would visit, and Malva, sobbing, would hug her. I had to restrain myself to keep from making fun of this Anna Karenina melodrama, which in my view differed from last century's drama only in that it was not as polished.

Roland rose to the rank of political activist. He concerned himself with his career and public image. Clearly he'd lost interest in his lover from the days of Sajudis. Maybe that's what Malva had in mind when she said, "I'm already encountering them." I realized that last winter the only time she saw Roland was on TV. She'd watch the tube, her mouth agape like a child's, as though she didn't recognize him, as though she couldn't believe that it was really he. I had trouble recognizing him too—I've already mentioned that I hadn't marked his features—a fitting figure in professional attire, for some reason speaking with a French accent. Was he the same person that Malva described holding the tricolor high as the rain drenched his face at the first Sajudis meeting? ("It was almost like tears, almost like fiercely gushing tears," according to Malva.) Malva greedily drank in the changes in Roland's appearance and behavior. Career potential makes even an unattractive man desirable, not to mention one who has what it takes arouse a woman's interest even without the achievement of a career. You couldn't say that they had fought or separated, or that their relationship had ended. They had simply seen each other less and less. Roland never called Malva—he said that he didn't have the time—and Malva could never get through to him. His secretary would answer his calls with a bell-like "What is this in reference to?" He was chauffeured to and from work in a government car. In any crowd or organized gathering he was constantly surrounded by functionaries. Malva still haunted public meetings and demonstrations, keeping her eyes on the Parliament building, hoping to catch a glimpse of her lover with the collar of his windbreaker flipped up and his hands shoved into his pockets.

Julia returned to Lithuania, but she no longer lived with me. She rented an apartment in the Old Town. As promised, she provided me with all kinds of vehicles, wheels, crutches, canes, even a special toilet that lowers itself when you sit down and raises itself to facilitate standing up when you press the foot-pedal. I marveled at the equipment and was a bit ashamed: This concern with bodily comforts seemed a little abnormal. Later I got used to it, and, secretly, I was even pleased.

Sporadically before Julia's return, and frequently afterward, strange telephone calls began to disturb me. The caller was a complete stranger. From his voice he seemed to be a youngish man. The first time I answered the phone, I heard an uneasy shout:

"Just don't hang up! Just don't hang up!"

"Okay," I answered, "I won't."

There was silence for quite a few minutes, I heard only a rustle.

"Excuse me," I said, becoming impatient, suddenly suspecting that a KGB official was trying to hook up to my phone, "I don't believe we had an appointment. How long do I have to listen to your breathing?"

"Please forgive me, ma'am. Forgive me. Of course, this call must seem strange to you, maybe even suspicious. But please try to understand. Please listen to me. I'm alone, completely alone. I haven't left my room for almost a year. I keep my window shades drawn and haven't seen sunlight in days. Now I'm afraid to look; I might pass out or go blind. I'm afraid of people. My neighbors bring me food, but I'm afraid of them. I know I need to conquer this fear, but how? That's why I'm calling you. We'll talk, and I'll become comfortable with the human voice. Next I'll try to accustom myself to the human face, gestures, and expressions."

"But why me? Do you know anything about me?"

"I found your name in the telephone book. It's a woman's maiden name, and you've got an apartment already. That means that you're not married, but you're no spring chicken. I've dialed the number a few times to make sure a man or child doesn't answer. You live alone, so I thought you'd understand me. Everyone else is so busy all the time. I just barely start talking and they call me a psycho case and hang up."

We talked for almost half an hour. He talked; I listened. The next time he called, the conversation turned to the metaphysical, and to God, in Whom back then it was forbidden to believe, and in Whom now it's almost impossible to believe.

The third time, he mentioned our compatriots who had escaped to the West and asked whether, given the opportunity to flee, I would take advantage of it. He said he would take the first flight West and never look back. He seemed to be trying to provoke me. He described his thoughts and goals with utmost candor, as if inviting me to do the same.

"What do you think about Kondrotas? Guzzling his German beer. Or that Baronas. He received a death sentence from Soviet courts, but he keeps publishing his little books and lining his pockets with dollars."*

I answered everything ambiguously, at times babbling meaninglessly, because I really had begun to suspect that the calls were not coincidental—that some provocateur was probing me. After Julia's return from America, the calls became more frequent, and I realized that my suspicions were well founded. I warned Julia not to get involved in any conversations with suspect loners on the telephone. Julia, although irritated, inquired about the

---

*Saulius Tomas Kondrotas and Aloyzas Baronas are Lithuanian writers who emigrated to the West.

conversations: What were they about; were the pauses frequent; was there a pattern to the calls; did they occur at a particular time or randomly? I thought that she might have had a similar experience.

"So you suspect it's a KGB agent?" Julia finally asked.

"Yes."

"But I don't understand the point of his pursuing you. Could you be dangerous to the Soviets?"

"You are. They want to recruit me to observe you and pass along the information."

Julia wrinkled her brow and asked seemingly meaningless questions about the timbre of the caller's voice and the pacing of his breaths. I said:

"All along one thing amazed me: Why was he so nervous? But I decided that he was probably inexperienced or new at the job."

"Here's another explanation," said Julia, "a completely nonpolitical one. What you've just described fits the behavior of a person who talks on the telephone while masturbating. Such perversions do exist. A friend of mine in America happens to be interested in precisely these questions, and she has told me quite a bit about it. I've even read a statement by a patient who practices this kind of behavior. It's very similar to your situation. Even the references to traveling abroad to foreign lands or warmer climates. It's a kind of code, signifying a desire to break out, to overcome one's vices."

Malva meanwhile had become unbearable. When Julia rented an apartment in the Old Town, Malva set up shop there too. Roland stopped by once in a while, but not because he missed Malva. He came to see Julia on business. Julia and I often consulted on how to help Malva.

"Her love affair with Roland is all in her head," Julia said. "He simply didn't dare to reject a woman who was offering herself as his lover. When I did Malva the favor of introducing them, it was obvious to me that although

Malva is by far my superior in the looks department, Roland would have preferred a date with me. It's because I'm American, and in this country that means something. But unfortunately, politicians from oppressed countries don't do a thing for me."

Until then I hadn't thought of Julia as vain. Later, it became clear that her pretensions and expectations were of a mammoth scale.

"It seems that the whole world's to blame because the Lithuanians aren't driving around in Mercedes-Benzes or studying abroad in Paris," she said. "The world doesn't owe you a thing."

"How should I put it? To a certain degree, yes, it is to blame, and yes, it does owe us something."

"Then God the Father is equally to blame."

"Probably God the Father too."

Julia wasn't religious. I was a believer, though she knew the tenets of Christianity better than I. She expected me to fall apart at the suggestion that God was first and foremost to blame for the injustices of the world, that it was He who had allowed them to occur. This was the first time I had disliked Julia. I thought, "Look, she came to Lithuania, had some interesting experiences, and collected the data she needed for her academic project while making some money on her articles describing current events. For a while longer she'll bum around the crumbling Old Town, sneering at our vision of the Athens of the North, and then she'll go back to her rich, satiated, emotionless America." But then I remembered the time she walked me to church and sat down by the gate next to a beggar. While I prayed, she talked to the miserable man, asking him how he'd come to be a beggar. She later gave him twenty-five rubles for interrupting his begging.

When Julia described various front- and backstage events in Parliament, she often used a term unfamiliar to me: "all these perversions." "Perversion" was not in the dictionary of foreign words and phrases. I didn't dare inquire about it—Julia used the word so naturally and assuredly, as if everyone should know it. I imagined that it referred to something not very good, not very nice, not very appropriate, even not very decent. I'm not sure what it was in our life that her foreigner's eye perceived as perverse. And, as I've already mentioned, I really didn't understand what the word meant. It's not our fault that Lithuanians don't always understand the virtues and vices as defined by the so-called civilized world; I wish that these "civilized" people and their pretentious words with no Lithuanian equivalents would stay at home. It's as if they're observing our every move under a microscope, but all they notice is the confusion of the swarming crowd demonstrating—the chants, the swaying left to right, while we smile and discuss our feelings.

Now I'll finish Malva's story.

She didn't show her face for a long time after the day I reminded her a second time about the rules of civility. She had snapped that it was probably love itself that I detested. Then in early fall, Malva knocked at my door. Although she had a key, she waited for me to answer and stood there hanging her head. I invited her in.

"It's over," she said, "I know that I was nothing but a plaything for Roland."

She began to cry, her shoulders heaving, but it was clear that these were just remnants of her pain: She'd already adjusted.

"It couldn't have been otherwise," I said. "The worst of it is that it took you so long to figure it out."

"Why couldn't it have been otherwise?" Malva turned her swollen, teary face to me. Her face had shrunk, resembling a child's. "Why couldn't it have been otherwise?"

And her eyes filled with tears.

I had made a grave error saying that it couldn't have been otherwise. I thought it would make things easier for her if she understood the scale of impossibility, but through her sobs, Malva pointed out that it *could* have been otherwise. One by one, she enumerated the mistakes that had determined everything. Julia was right—Roland had never loved Malva and would have preferred fooling around with an exotic American, but Malva wouldn't have been able to bear this news. She was consoling herself with the notion that Roland had at least loved her at some point.

I made us supper—milk soup. Malva sipped her soup, childishly slurping up the noodle hanging from her spoon. She asked me to sprinkle on some sugar. Poor girl! I realized that I loved her and would forgive all her whims and caprices and her ignoring what I called "rules of civility." But I had no idea how to help her, what to advise. We turned on the TV. A crowd of people rejoicing. Victory. The camera operator focused on the pure cold sky. A spattering of clouds—lonely, scattered, but unusually dark, almost black—were stirring above the square. Malva's eyes searched the screen, hoping for a glimpse of Roland. He wasn't there. We went to bed late that night. Malva fell asleep right away. I, dressed in pajamas, sat down in the wheelchair given to me by Julia—she'd already gone back to America—and wheeled myself up and down the length of the room.

Translated from the Lithuanian
by Jura Avizienis

Glossary

barricade—defensive obstruction, hastily built, as in a street

bigotry—intolerant dedication to one's own unfounded beliefs or opinions of persons or groups

bizarre—notably strange or odd in appearance or in style

bureaucracy—government notable for red tape and rigidity of rules

calamity—major misfortune or disaster causing lasting distress

censorship—the banning or suppression of anything considered objectionable, as books, motion pictures

chameleon—species of lizard able to change the color of its skin according to its immediate surroundings

coercion—the act of compelling by intimidation or threat

coif—tight-fitting cap worn under the veil by women of religious orders

contaminate—to soil, infect, or pollute with something unclean

counterfeit—to make a false copy of, especially money

demagogue—person who seeks to gain power through false claims or promises

demobilization—the process of discharging or releasing from military service

detox—(short form of detoxification) to free the body of an addictive or poisonous substance

dissident—one who disagrees with or actively opposes the political or religious system

drought—period of absence of rainfall, prolonged enough to prevent successful growing of crops

emigration—act of leaving one's home country to settle in another country

ephemeral—passing; lasting for only a short time

epitome—embodiment; typical example of a class of objects

ethnicity—racial, tribal, or cultural origin or background

famine—prolonged, serious shortage of food, conducive to starvation

futility—uselessness of effort; ineffectiveness

geek—(slang) person who is socially inept or outside the mainstream

harmonious—musically agreeable; acting in accord with others

KGB—initials of the Russian name of the former secret police of the Soviet Union

lesbian—female who prefers another female as a sexual partner

liquidate—to break up or do away with; to kill; to settle financial accounts

mainstream—principal course or trend of activities

nationalism—strong devotion to a nation, especially as opposed to other nations

phenomenon—fact or event that can be observed; something remarkable or extraordinary

pirogi—dough filled with a spicy filling, as meat or cheese

pluralism—social system in which diverse groups participate harmoniously

radiation—emission of radiant energy in particles or waves

slander—spoken defamation of a person; as opposed to libel, or written defamation

shadow cabinet—leaders of the opposition in a parliamentary form of government

stalemate—contest that results in a tie; position in which no party can move

subservient—subordinate; submissive

subsidy—grant of money by a state to a private person or company

surveillance—close watch kept over a person or a place

tacky—in poor taste; of inferior quality

Further Reading

General Soviet

Amalrik, Andrei. *Notes of a Revolutionary*. New York: Alfred Knopf, 1982. These are the personal memoirs of a stubborn defender of human rights in the USSR from 1965 to 1980, regularly sentenced to prison or exile, only to return as a thorn in the Soviet side.

Antonov-Ovseyenko, Anton. *The Time of Stalin: Portrait of a Tyranny*. New York: Harper and Row, 1981. The son of an important Bolshevik leader gives an inside view of the Stalin regime. The author survived years in prisons and concentration camps and saw the assassination of his father during a Stalin "purge."

Massie, Robert K. *Nicholas and Alexandra: An Intimate Account of the Last of the Romanovs and the Fall of Imperial Russia*. New York: Atheneum, 1967. Tsar Nicholas was influenced in his rule by the bizarre hypnotist Rasputin. Massie weaves the tale of how the unresponsive government that Nicholas was persuaded to maintain led inevitably to the overthrow of tsarist Russia.

Medvedev, Roy. *The October Revolution*. New York: Columbia University, 1979. This treatment of the Bolsheviks discusses both their triumph in the revolution and their ill-founded policies that brought ruin to the country.

Orlova, Raisa. *Memoirs*. New York: Random House, 1983. Trusted by the Soviets to be interpreter of foreign culture to the Russian people, Orlova was involved in the elite circle of Soviet intelligentsia. Here she tells what she saw and how she became disillusioned to the point of resigning from the Party in 1980.

Sharansky, Natan. *Fear No Evil*. New York: Random House, 1988. Sharansky spent nine years in a KGB prison to which he was sentenced for helping Russian Jews who wished to emigrate to Israel. This is his story.

Solzhenistsyn, Aleksandr. *The Oak and the Calf: Sketches of Literary Life in the Soviet Union*. New York: Harper and Row, 1979. One of the world's current master novelists gives a personal account of his ten-year battle with the Soviet government to get his writing published in his native country.

Armenia

Bauer, Elisabeth, and Jacob Schmidheim. *Armenia: Past and Present*. Lucerne: Reich Verlag, 1981. A history of the Armenians, from ancient times to the nationalist struggle against the Soviets.

Lang, David Marshall. *The Armenians, a People in Exile*. Boston: Allen & Unwin, 1981. Lang grapples with the changes that Soviet rule brought to Armenia.

Azerbaijan

Altstadt, Audrey L. *The Azerbaijani Turks: Power and Destiny Under Russian Rule.* Stanford: Hoover, 1992. A recent history of Azerbaijan, beginning in ancient Media and culminating in Black January, 1991, when it declared independence from the USSR.

Belarus

Zaprudnik, Jan. *Belarus: At a Crossroads in History.* Boulder: Westview Press, 1993. An up-to-date look at the people of Belarus and their struggle for freedom, which continues even now that the USSR is defunct.

Estonia

Kung, Andras. *A Dream of Freedom.* Cardiff, GB: Boreas, 1980. Kung lauds the courage of Baltic peoples during four decades of Russian imperialism.

Raun, Taivo. *Estonia and the Estonians.* Stanford: Hoover, 1991. The history of Estonia is traced from prehistoric times, through the Soviet period and into the age of *glasnost* and *perestroika.* Estonia has long been a sought-after prize in power struggles among world leaders.

Georgia

Rosen, Roger. *Introduction to the Georgian Republic.* Hong Kong: Odyssey, 1991. Illustrated with maps and color photos, this comprehensive book guides the reader through the history, land, and cultures of Georgia.

Suny, Ronald Grigor. *The Making of the Georgian Nation.* Bloomington: Indiana University Press, 1988. A concise overview of the history of the Georgian peoples, from their ethnogenesis in the 1st millenium BC, ending with a thorough analysis of the Soviet period.

Kazakhstan

Cosman, Catherine. *Conflicts in the Soviet Union: The Untold Story of Kazakhstan.* New York: Human Rights Watch, 1990. Covering the period from 1985 to 1990, Cosman uncovers persecution, racism, and irresponsible politics in Kazakhstan.

Olcott, Martha Brill. *The Kazakhs.* Stanford: Hoover, 1987. In the·steppes of Central Asia live the Islamic Kazakhs. Olcott traces the growth of the Kazakh nation, its colonization by Soviet Russia, and the struggle to regain autonomy.

Kyrgyzstan

Hatto, A.T. *The Memorial Feast for Kokotoy-Khan.* New York: Oxford, 1977. The national epic of Kyrgyzstan, origin legend to the Kyrgyz people, is translated into English alongside the Kyrgyz original.

Latvia

Bilmanis, Alfred. *A History of Latvia*. Westport, Conn: Greenwood Press, 1970. Bilmanis follows the roots of the Latvian people from ancient times. Includes maps.

Mikhailov, Nikolai Leontevich. *The Amber Republic*. Riga: Liesma, 1976. This overview of Lithuania includes history, maps, and descriptions of the land and people.

Lithuania

Vardys, Vytas Stanley. *The Catholic Church, Dissent, and Nationality in Soviet Lithuania*. New York: Columbia University Press, 1978. Catholics were not allowed to practice their religion freely under Soviet rule. Vardys explains the historical details and how this human rights violation led to the nationalist movement in Lithuania.

Wolfe, George M. *Once Upon a Time in Rossein*. Sarasota, FL: Wolfe, 1976. These personal memoirs describe what it was like to grow up Jewish in Raseiniai, Lithuania, under Soviet rule.

Moldova

Dailey, Erika. *Human Rights in Moldova*. New York: Helsinki Watch, 1993. The Dniester River region is the focus of this civil rights investigation, explaining the struggles of nationalism.

Dima, Nicholas. *From Moldavia to Moldova: The Soviet-Romanian Territorial Dispute*. Boulder: East European Monographs, 1991. The recent power struggles are explained in the context of history, ethnic identity, culture, language, and politics.

Russia

Salisbury, Harrison F. *The 900 Days: The Siege of Leningrad*. New York: Harper and Row, 1969. The Nazis seized Leningrad in October, 1941, and held it for six winter months, killing nearly two million people. Salisbury explores the disturbing possibility that Stalin allowed it to happen.

Smith, Hedrick. *The Russians*. New York: Ballantine, 1976. The author, who spent four years among the Russians, articulately conveys the heart and soul of a nation.

Smith, Hedrick. *The New Russians*. New York: Avon, 1991. Fifteen years after his best-selling Soviet portrait, *The Russians*, Smith tells the astonishing story of the modern revolution, the breakdown of the USSR, and the rise of Boris Yeltsin.

Tajikistan

Conflict in the Soviet Union: Tajikistan. New York: Human Rights Watch, 1991. This is a revealing short book on civil rights violations and persecution in Tajikistan.

Rakowska-Harmstone, Teresa. *Russia and Nationalism in Central Asia: The Case of Tadzhikistan.* Baltimore: Johns Hopkins, 1970. The development of nationalism in Tajikistan is considered, as well as how the Soviets reacted to it.

Turkmenistan

Maslow, Jonathan. *Sacred Horses: Memoirs of a Turkmen Cowboy.* New York: Random House, 1994. Maslow traveled in Turkmenistan, and these are his observations of the people he met there and their current situation.

Ukraine

Dushnyck, Walter. *Fifty Years Ago.* New York, 1983. In 1932-33 a famine was intentionally created in Ukraine as a Stalinist move to decimate the population. Dushnyck considers the causes and consequences of this atrocity.

Uzbekistan

Allworth, Edward A. *The Modern Uzbeks, from the 14th Century to the Present.* Stanford: Hoover, 1990. The Uzbeks, most of whom are Muslims, comprise the third-largest people in the former USSR. This history discusses their relationship with the Soviet government and how they have dealt with religious persecution..

Glazebrook, Philip. *Journey to Kiva.* London: Harvill, 1992. The reader is invited to meet the people and places of Uzbekistan.

Index

Index